Floral Design & Arrangement

Floral Design & Arrangement

GARY L. McDANIEL

RESTON PUBLISHING COMPANY, INC.

A Prentice-Hall Company

RESTON, VIRGINIA

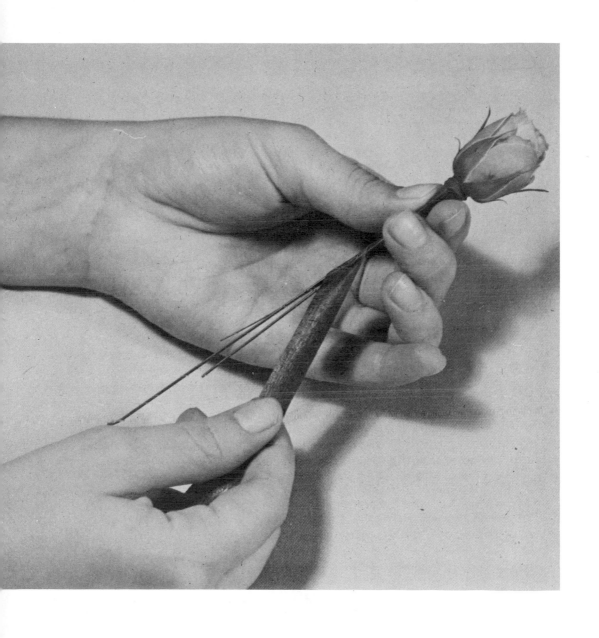

Library of Congress Cataloging in Publication Data

McDaniel, Gary L
    Floral design & arrangement.

    Includes index.
      1. Flower arrangement.   2. Design, Decorative.
I. Title.

SB449.M29   745.92   80-39555

ISBN 0-8359-2072-0

Table of Contents

to Judith

Preface

The field of commercial floral design in the United States provides a rewarding career for individuals who enjoy working with people and with flowers. Florists are using a high degree of skill and creativity in designs today from a greater variety of flower types than have been previously available. The floral design student who wishes to find employment as a floral designer will benefit from the combined training received from classroom instruction and practical experience.

This book was written to provide a basic instruction in the techniques of floral design. The author has attempted to describe the fundamental skills and methods used by florists when creating modern commercial designs. The beginning floral designer will then be able to develop these skills further in more advanced design work. The material is intended for use in introductory floral design courses at the secondary, vocational-technical school, or college levels. It is also intended to serve as a reference text for those individuals entering the commercial florist field who have received little previous training.

Unit I of the text presents the theoretical aspects of floral design. The influencing factors in the progress of the art of floral design are highlighted. The theory of floral design is described through a comprehensive discussion of the principles and elements of design. The specific skills needed for creating flower arrangements are presented for students who have no previous experience with cut-flower care and handling for designing.

The construction methods used for creating floral designs are described in Unit II. The techniques for constructing cut-flower arrangements in containers are discussed for the basic design styles. These are presented in order of skill required in their construction. Basic corsage construction is presented through step-by-step procedures required for the more common styles sold by florists. The use of dried and everlasting flowers in design is described for those students who will be exposed to this important facet of the business. Techniques for drying and preserving flowers and plant material are also explained for those persons who are interested in this aspect of floral designing.

The advanced student is provided a detailed description of commercial florists' designs in Unit III. Florists' holiday and seasonal arrangement styles are presented as a guideline for the students. The fundamental floral design styles and traditions for wedding arrangements and decorations are explained in detail. Wedding bouquet construction methods are described for several of the basic designs. The various types of floral arrangements for funerals are described and methods of construction are presented. The serious student of floral design will be able refer to these chapters long after the course is completed.

G. McD.

ACKNOWLEDGMENTS:

The author wishes to give special thanks to Mack M. Gentry, Curtis C. Hansard, and Regina Horne of the Knoxville Wholesale Florists, Inc., Knoxville, Tennessee, for their friendship and assistance in the use of their flowers and facilities during the preparation of this book.

Deepest thanks go also to my parents, Lester and Wilma McDaniel, for their assistance and suggestions during the preparation of this material. Their expertise and experience has been enhanced during more than thirty years of operating a retail flower shop. And especially I want to give my sincerest thanks to my wife, Judith, for her invaluable assistance and patience during the preparation of this book.

G. McD.

UNIT I:

Floral Design Theory

CHAPTER *1:*

A History of Floral Design Art

Flowers have adorned the earth since the beginning of civilization, giving it beauty, color, and function. Our earliest ancestors, the cave dwellers, must surely have wondered at the beauty and delicate fragrance of the wild flowers around them. Through the centuries, flowers have played an increasingly important role in the lives of people through their use in religion, home decoration, and personal adornment. Today, flowers are admired extensively in our homes, churches, and businesses. Flowers are used on special occasions to express the emotions of love, faith, and friendship and add their beauty to the home furnishings of our modern dwellings.

Knowledge of the floral arts of earlier cultures and civilizations is important so that the modern designer might better understand the derivation of the flower arrangement styles used today. The floral designer is often required to duplicate flower arrangements depicting a specific period or style of design to accompany a room decoration. Competitive designers may also be required to duplicate flower arrangements of specific periods of art history.

Floral designs, as we arrange them today, are a blending of two styles, Oriental and European. The basic European designs are known as *mass* arrangements. Floral artists of the various periods of continental European art history used lavish quantities of flower types and colors to create a massive display. The art of Oriental design emphasizes a type of simplicity that has become known as *line* design. Modern florists' designs incorporate the simplistic line from the Oriental art and the massed arrangements of European designs. Today's American floral pieces are called *line-mass* arrangements. The modern floral designer uses these skills to create designs that have more simplicity and originality than were present in the past.

THE CLASSICAL PERIOD OF FLORAL DESIGN

Egyptian Period (2800–28 B.C.)

The Egyptian civilization is one of the oldest known, yet much information is available concerning the use of flowers in the lives of these people. Archaeological excavations of ancient Egyptian tombs have revealed that flowers were an important aspect of these people's lives. From the paintings of the early ways of life on tomb walls, it is learned that containers such as vases, jars, and bowls were used to hold flowers. These containers were made from gold, polished alabaster, slate, and dark green diorite. Although porcelain was not made, the early Egyptians did produce a ware of finely ground silicate called faience.

The Egyptians favored wide-mouthed basins, which were fitted with devices for holding flowers or fruit. The bowls designed to hold flowers were constructed with holes around the rim where stems were placed to reach the water. Bronze containers were fitted with metal loops attached to the bottom and the sides through which flower stems were placed. Chaplets for the hair were constructed from lotus petals, buds, and leaves placed at the center of the forehead. The Egyptians used the primary colors of red, yellow, and blue predominantly in their designs. Flowers, fruit, and foliage were placed in regimented rows, allowing the colors to be sharply segregated.

The royal families of Egypt were ardent plant collectors, and their gardens displayed a wide variety of plant species. Egyptian flowers were so abundant that they were even exported into the Roman Empire. Among the flowers used by the ancient Egyptian people were water lilies, lotus, acacia, roses, violets, Madonna lilies, narcissus, poppies, and jasmine. Lotus flowers were often combined with fruit, other flowers, and foliage to create formal bouquets to be used as offerings to the gods or to the dead. A typical arrangement used to decorate a feast table consisted of fruits and vegetables neatly piled in low baskets. These arrangements were formed into a mounded design, topped by lotus blossoms, and edged by a symmetrical row of lotus petals or leaves.

Overall, the Egyptian style may best be described as having clarity and an orderly simplicity. Two basic artistic functions prevailed in these designs: *repetition and alternation*. With this style, a series of floral groups (flower, bud, and foliage), each exactly alike, were repeated in a pattern around the periphery of a design. Colors and heights of stems were also repeated in units in this manner.

Greek Period (600–146 B.C.)

During the period of the late Egyptian era, the Greek civilization was flourishing. The ancient Greeks were by nature a people so dedicated to beauty that their art heritage has lived through the ages. The Greeks did not arrange their flowers in vases or bouquets; rather, flowers were strewn on the ground during festivals and were made into garlands and wreaths to be worn or carried. Everyone wore wreaths for special occasions in ancient Greece. Wreaths symbolized allegiance and dedication, so they were presented to outstanding athletes or fashioned from flowers to be worn at festivals. Wreaths were placed on the heads of their heroes and important dignitaries, and on their statues of gods and goddesses. Funeral graves were decorated with garlands of roses, sweet marjoram, hyacinths, lilies, iris, narcissus, and violets. Lovers often fashioned fragrant wreaths and garlands of violets, thyme, berries, narcissus, or seed pods interspersed with leaves. The Greeks also wore flowers in their hair for personal adornment and beauty.

Wreaths were so much a part of the Greek tradition that books were written to describe the appropriate flowers, forms, and etiquette for wearing them. Flowers were so important in Greek culture that potted plants were grown indoors to supply the necessary plant materials. Florists were engaged to create garlands and wreaths to be used for gifts and decorations for special occasions.

The *cornucopia* (horn of plenty) was introduced by the Greek culture.

FIGURE 1–1 *The cornucopia or "horn-of-plenty" has been used for centuries as a symbol for abundance.*

It is associated with the Greek god Zeus, who was nursed and reared by a goat known as Amalthaea. In gratitude for this, Zeus placed Amalthaea among the stars and her horn then became a symbol for abundance. The Greeks always placed flowers, fruits, and vegetables in the cornucopia in its upright position, rather than on its side spilling its contents as it is displayed today (see Figure 1–1).

The floral designs of the ancient Greeks were limited by rituals and traditions. Symbolic association dominated almost every aspect of their lives. Each flower was connected with a god or hero and was loved for its particular character. The flowers, fragrance, and symbolism were foremost in their designs and color was not a consideration. The Greek heritage of simplicity and grace in design has survived the centuries.

Roman Period (28 B.C.–A.D. 325)

The Roman civilization contributed little new in the use of flowers, but continued the earlier customs of the Greeks. By the second century of its existence, the Roman civilization became more luxurious. Their use of plant material became more elaborate, often reaching preposterous proportions. Their extravagant love of flowers is exemplified by their customary use of roses at evening banquets. Here roses were often strewn on the floor to a depth of two feet, while rose petals and other flowers rained from the ceiling. The fragrance from these floral heaps is said to have been suffocating.

The blossom-filled scarf became traditional during this period. Flowers were carried on a scarf and offered at an altar as a part of Roman religious ceremonies. The use of wreaths and garlands was continued from the Greeks. These were often more elaborate than the Greek prototypes, with wreaths forming high crowns and coming to a point over the forehead. Garlands were even more elaborate, with the centers being widest and tapering toward each end.

Although the Romans' major contribution to floral art was the perfection of the garland, there is also evidence that flowers were actually arranged in containers. Flowers were placed in a *liknon* (basket), which was high at the back and flattened in front. A typical floral arrangement of the classical Roman style would be placed in a liknon. The flowers are placed low between feathery branches so that their silhouettes are clearly visible. This requires adequate spacing of the branches. Flowers used in these arrangements were always highly fragrant and bright in color.

The Byzantine Period (A.D. 320–600)

Following the fall of the Roman Empire, the traditions of this civilization were preserved for a time in the Byzantine art of the Near East. Greek and Roman flower usage styles were continued, but the garland was constructed differently. These were often composed of narrow bands of fruit or flowers alternating with foliage and given a twisted effect.

The Byzantine culture provided a major contribution to floral art with the introduction of symmetrical, stylized tree compositions. Containers were filled with foliage to resemble symmetrical, conical trees. These were decorated at regular intervals with clusters of flowers or fruit. These tree compositions were placed in baskets or large goblets having scroll-shaped handles.

Another style of the Byzantine era was the placement of a central stem rising from a low container. Pairs of leaves, flowers, or fruit were bound to it at intervals on either side in perfect balance to create a stylized artificial plant. This design tapered to the top and was composed of a series of twin flowers having bright colors.

An authentic Byzantine arrangement may be created in a container filled with dark and light foliage interspersed with small lilies, star-shaped flowers, and bunches of grapes. The leaves are packed closely together to provide a rigid form. These spires of foliage are wound facing and balancing each other on each side of a central stem. Flowers and fruit are spaced at regular intervals. The most common color schemes used in these designs consisted of neighboring hues (such as green, blue-green, blue, and violet) with accents of their complements (red, red-orange, orange, and yellow). Containers used for this style of design were elegant and often possessed nearly pointed bases.

The Middle Ages (A.D. 476–1400)

The Middle Ages occurred after the fall of the western Roman Empire and before a resurgence of the arts during the Renaissance. Very little is known of the floral art of this period. Most of our information comes from the artistry shown in Persian paintings, rugs, and tapestries of the fourteenth century.

Persian art shows flowers arranged in vases. Persian rugs from this period show the use of analogous, monochromatic, and triadic color schemes in floral designs having an Oriental influence. These rugs depict narcissus, carnations, and tulips arranged in symmetrical groups in flat Chinese flasks. Holes were provided at the surface of the containers to admit sprays of foliage and flowers.

Persian paintings depict more gracefulness and informality in their floral designs. These were created to show a natural appearance using bunches of carnations, roses, and tulips, with tall lily blooms above. Short-stemmed blossoms were often arranged in symmetrical balance and topped by a taller-stemmed lily, iris, or rose. Branches from flowering shrubs were also placed in containers to create "single-flower" bouquets.

Floral designs were created in containers of Chinese porcelain, flat bottles, flasks, gourd shapes with fitted spouts, and pear-shaped vases. A commonly used container was a flask having a rounded profile with a short neck. It was decorated with birds and placed on a metal base with feet of crouching lions and armlike wings of a dragon. The sides of the flask were fitted with openings to admit flower stems. These containers with the flowers were placed either on a low, small table or on a small rug directly on the floor for viewing.

EUROPEAN PERIODS OF FLORAL DESIGN

The Renaissance Period (A.D. 1400–1600)

The Renaissance style was established first in Italy and then spread throughout continental Europe and influenced the development of their cultures during this period. The Renaissance style was patterned after the classical styles of Greece and Rome and brought a rebirth to floral design.

Characteristic floral arrangements of the Renaissance were very large, tall, symmetrically balanced, and pyramidal in form. Flowers were arranged so that they were about twice the height of the container and in an uncrowded, loose, and airy fashion. Intense colors were used so that flowers created a contrast with the white plastered walls of homes and buildings. Brilliant colors were combined in a triadic (three-color) color scheme.

A traditional Renaissance floral design would be constructed in a container such as a red Venetian glass vase, metal pedestal vase, or a wide-mouthed marble urn. The arrangement is then styled from light, airy flowers into a tight, formal bouquet using such flowers of the period as dainty carnations (pinks), daisies, lily-of-the-valley, small fruits (most often grape bunches), cones, and foliage. Other plant materials available at the time that were used in floral arrangements were lilies, violets, roses, primroses, iris, and anemone with the foliage of olive, ivy, and laurel used as a contrast in these designs. Many traditional floral designs created today are styled from the Renaissance arrangements, such as the Christmas wreaths of fruit, cones, and flowers. Renaissance floral design is quite suitable today for use as a stage or church arrangement, particularly when a marble base is used to emphasize the massive design.

FIGURE 1–2
*A modern interpretation of
a traditional Hogarthian curve design.*

The Baroque Period (A.D. 1600–1775)

The Italian artist Michelangelo greatly influenced the artistic transition from the classical Renaissance style to the lavish mood of the Baroque period. Although the Baroque styles of floral design began in Italy, their concepts were slowly adopted by other artists of Europe and became most highly developed by the painters of Holland and Belgium.

These arrangements were often created as symmetrical, oval-shaped designs early in the Baroque period, but asymmetrical curves in the shape of an S or a crescent were later adopted. The S curve was created by an English painter named William Hogarth, who described this style as being "the line of beauty." This style of flower arrangement, the Hogarthian curve, is still quite popular in modern design because it utilizes a rhythmic, asymmetrical balance (see Figure 1–2).

These designs were generally rather tall with an abundance of different flower types and colors used together in the same arrangement. When the curved asymmetrical designs evolved, this massive style was refined to one of graceful, dynamic movement with an elegant appearance. Color was used in an unrestrained manner in the Baroque designs. The use of many different and bright colors in these floral arrangements was done to enhance the otherwise dull-gray interior walls of the homes during this period of history.

This heavy, massive bouquet style required large containers for support. Some common containers used for these floral pieces were constructed from metal, stone, pottery, or heavy glass. The designs were arranged from such flowers as iris, marigold, lily, peony, canna, narcissus, hollyhock, and roses. These designs also incorporated many types of accessories, such as figurines, fans, and butterflies, to create a composition suitable for the Baroque artists.

The Flemish Style (A.D. 1600–1750)

The development of the Baroque design style had its greatest impact in Belgium (Flanders) and Holland. Traditional Baroque styles were refined by the old masters as they created floral designs for their paintings. These arrangements were not as loose and open as in the contemporary Baroque style, but were better proportioned and more compact. Tulips were used profusely and were combined with a large array of other flower types into massed, oval-shaped bouquets (see Figure 1–3). In this design style, the flowers were usually taller than the height of the container. Generally, the basic concepts of the Baroque style were continued with these adaptations in the Flemish style of floral design.

The French Tradition of Floral Design

The French styles for decorating and flower arranging were changed as often as the country changed political situations. There are four basic French periods with which contemporary flower arrangers are concerned: (1) French Baroque, (2) French Rococo, (3) Louis XVI, and (4) Empire. Although the artistic styles created during these periods are designated as French in origin, their characteristics were copied throughout Europe, England, and in the New World.

French Baroque (seventeenth century): The development of the Baroque style of design was advanced during the reign of King Louis XIV of France. He was dedicated to the idea that a great king should influence

FIGURE 1–3 *The Flemish designs were more compact and better proportioned than early arrangement styles.*

the development of all the arts. He appointed a state secretary of fine arts to regulate the activities of scores of artists and craftsmen. Under his direction, a grandiose palace and gardens, called the Chateau de Versailles, was built to become the center for court life and artistic creation in France. Although the cost of the construction of the Chateau de Versailles and employment of his artists, together with the costs of war and allied extravagances, eventually depleted the treasury of France, there is little doubt that Louis XIV was primarily responsible for establishing a true French national style.

The French Baroque style of floral design was directly influenced by traditional Baroque art, but certain features make it purely French in origin. The court society during the reign of Louis XIV had become idle and effeminate with extravagant tastes for luxury. Feminine appeal became an important characteristic of the floral designs of this period in France.

An important design style that has survived since this period was the *topiary*. The topiary ball or topiary tree has its beginnings in the formal trimmed evergreen topiary trees that were typical in the French gardens. Flower arrangements were of the bouquet form, with little thought given to design by the arrangers. Symmetry of design was found in these arrangements, with the largest flower types being used at the outer edges. No grouping of kinds or colors of flowers was used and no center of interest was created in these designs.

French Rococo (eighteenth century): During the reign of King Louis XV of France, the national styles were dictated by his mistress Antoinette Poisson, Marquise de Pompadour. Although her interest and support of the arts was directly responsible for draining the French treasury, she had an everlasting impact on the development of the arts. Under her guidance and influence, the informal designs of the French Baroque era gave way to the more formal, feminine designs that developed into the French Rococo period. These floral arrangements were predominantly asymmetrical and curvilinear in form, with the crescent (C curve) used more often than the Hogarthian curve (S style).

The term *Rococo—rock and shell style—*is taken from the use of graceful arcs that formed the dominant lines of these designs. Flowers found in Rococo style designs were very delicate and airy. The predominant colors were subtle rather than contrasting. The most popular colors used during this period were apricot, peach, cream, rose-gray, sage-green, yellow, beige, turquoise, and powder blue. Containers consisted of Dresden china, bisque, alabaster, Venetian glass, silver, and bronze in the form of compotes, vases, bowls, and urns. Delicate accessories were included to enhance these designs in the form of dainty porcelain figurines, lace fans, and blackened-eye masks.

Louis XVI (late eighteenth century): The period of French art history during the short reign of Louis XVI showed a continued movement to femininity in design styles. This was the result of the queen's direction in setting court styles. Marie Antoinette favored delicate, cool colors highlighted with gold and she disdained the overly lavish containers of previous French styles.

Following the French Revolution in 1789, a new movement in art evolved which was inspired by the rediscovery of the buried Roman ruins of Pompeii and Herculaneum. With this movement came a revival of the classical styles of design. This period has been called the *Classical Revival Period*—or *Neoclassical Period*—of design. The design styles of Europe, England, and America were greatly influenced by this Neoclassicism during the early years of the nineteenth century.

Empire (1804–14): Nowhere else in the western world were Neoclassical styles used as they were during the period that Napoleon Bonaparte was emperor of France. Under the guidance of two of his court architects, Perier and Fontaine, the Empire design style was created. These were characterized by masculine designs featuring dramatic, militaristic themes. Napolean dictated the styles that were used and femininity was dropped from the French designs.

Empire arrangements were often rather massive in size and weight and displayed obvious symbolism. Emblems and symbols, such as replicas of sphinxes, lions, and other military symbols, were used to enhance the designs. Napoleon's trademarks of the letter N, the bee, and the Empire star were also often included in designs. Containers were heavy and constructed of marble, porcelain, bisque, or metal. These were often shaped like a beehive and stood on feet shaped like those of a bear, or they also may have incorporated a golden lion somewhere in their design.

Flower arrangements of the Empire era were more compact than those of earlier French periods, with simple lines in a triangular shape and strong color contrasts. A typical Empire design would be arranged in a heavy urn containing an abundance of large, richly colored flowers. The arrangement might be draped with garlands and would contain some symbolism denoting militarism or Napoleon influence. This design would be displayed upon a marble-topped pedestal to portray the masculine feeling of the Empire period.

The English Georgian Period (1714–60)

The Baroque period spanned the reigns of the English kings George I and George II, so this period of art in England is referred to as the Georgian period. The floral designs of the Baroque style were influenced greatly by the Chinese arts, which acquired much interest during this period of active trading between Europe and the Orient. The Baroque style utilized massed arrangements of flowers that were crammed into wide-mouthed containers with little design being applied. The Chinese style was incorporated in Georgian arrangements by the creation of symmetrical forms, usually triangular-shaped floral designs. The all-white or monochromatic color scheme was popularized, but rich color schemes were also used. The textural quality of these arrangements was velvety, with only a single flower type used most often.

During the later years of the Georgian period, floral designs reflected the movement away from formality and symmetry. The nosegay (tuzzy-muzzy), or hand-held bouquet, became stylish. Small neck pieces and hairpieces were fashioned from flowers to be worn as a proper accessory for fashionable ladies. Small nosegay-type bouquets were placed in bowls for display on tables in both formal and informal settings. These small bouquets were the first use of table centerpieces as we know them today. Fragrance was the most important prerequisite for flowers selected for these small bouquets because it was thought their perfume would help to prevent diseases.

The Victorian Period (1820–1901)

At no time in history was the use of flowers considered to be so fashionable as it was during the reign of Queen Victoria of England. During this era, floral designs were generally poorly proportioned. Large masses of flowers were placed tightly into a container to create a compact arrangement. These designs were usually asymmetrical. No definite focal point was created and many different colors were placed randomly throughout the design.

With the increasing wealth and power of the middle classes in England during the late nineteenth century, little restraint was applied to design and flower arrangements were grossly overdone. Artificial flowers were created from feathers, wax, shells, and paper for use in arrangements. These were often so dainty that they were placed under glass domes for protection and display. Flowers were even created from the hair of dead relatives and were arranged in frames. Dried flowers were also designed in framed arrangements and were of such good quality that some can be found in museums today.

The typical flower arrangement of the Victorian period would have an asymmetrical balance and a massed, tightly compact effect. No definite style of arrangement is prevalent from this period since the designs were often blendings of the current trends in art of previous periods. The flowers were arranged in elaborate containers on short stems and so tightly packed that an airless appearance resulted. So many different colors and flower types were used together that the entire arrangement often appeared spotted and unplanned.

Near the end of the Victorian period, an age noted for its general lack of artistic taste, serious attempts were made to establish rules for flower arranging. It had become recognized that art was required in the basic techniques of design, so the art of flower arrangement was taught by skilled designers. It was considered an important decorative art and many people studied the techniques of flower arrangement seriously. This recognition of the skills required in the creation of successful designs helped to establish flower arranging as a professional art as practiced by modern professional florists.

AMERICAN PERIODS OF FLORAL DESIGN

Early American Period (1620–1720)

The early colonists brought to America the styles of the Renaissance; but in the beginning, they had little time to devote to the frivolity of art and flower arranging. These colonists were avid gardeners, though their efforts were directed at providing food and herbs for medicine. The first settlers who came to New England were not members of the aristocracy, but rather Puritans who were seeking religious freedom.

Once the early colonists had established their settlements and provided for their well-being, there was time to turn to the beautification of their surroundings. Since they were unable to bring fancy floral vases and decorative containers with them from England, the Puritans used common household utensils to hold their flowers that were gathered from the wild. Common containers used for holding flowers were copper and pewter kettles, pans, and serving ware and pottery pitchers. There was little evidence of color grouping or design in these arrangements; rather they were created with simplicity and charm. Dried materials, such as grasses, wheat, cattails, honesty, and thistles, were characteristically used in these massed, informal arrangements.

Colonial Williamsburg Period (1714–80)

By the time Williamsburg was established as the capital of the Virginia colonies, life had eased into that of sophistication and culture. Active

FIGURE 1–4   *A traditional Colonial Williamsburg design.*

trade with England, continental Europe, and Asia was possible, and the cultural characteristics and artistic styles from these areas were adapted in the New World art. The Rococo period and English Georgian design styles were blended into what we call the Colonial Williamsburg design of flower arrangement. The arrangements created in the southern colonial tradition were apparently copied from floral prints of the European painters and from tapestries shipped to the colonists. Some even included Chinese vases and figurines into their designs.

The Colonial Williamsburg flower arrangement was of the massed bouquet design, although the flowers were arranged with ample space between them to allow a casual, open appearance. Designs were styled in the fan shape or were rectangular in shape, but the most common was the globular or round arrangement (see Figure 1–4). These were constructed so that the flowers were lightly arranged at the top, while those with more visual weight were placed close above the rim of the container, sometimes completely concealing it. The height of the arrangement varied from one to several times the height of the container. Dried flowers and grasses were often included in these designs with accessories of fruit and flowers placed on the table around the container. The Colonial Williamsburg floral design style is highly copied today for use in decorating homes using the southern colonial tradition.

American Federal Period (1780–1820)

The floral art of the American Federal period took its styles from the Neoclassic and Empire designs that evolved in Europe at that time. It became a distinct style in America as the colonies received their independence. The American people wanted to break away from the traditions of England and desired to create their own national art styles. These floral designs were influenced most by the delicate French style, with the individual beauty of the flowers being stressed. In these designs, the height of the flowers was greater than the width of the arrangement. The floral designs were little different than those found in the Neoclassic movement and gradually gave way to the ornate and stuffy designs characteristic of the Victorian period.

HISTORY OF ORIENTAL FLOWER ARRANGING

While the floral art of the Western world was developing along the lines of massed arrangements, the Oriental art of floral design was developing in an entirely different manner. The Oriental art style originated the use of asymmetrical balance and proportion in floral designs. Western styles were influenced by Oriental design following the opening of trade routes with the Orient by Dutch and English merchants in the seventeenth century.

The Chinese Style

The use of flowers and plant materials as adornment was first practiced as a part of religious ceremonies by the Buddhist priests of India, where this religious sect originated. These priests disdained the sacrifice of living plants for use of adornment, so only storm-broken branches and stems were scattered on Buddhist altars or were placed in pottery urns as decoration. The Chinese continued the practice of decorating the altars of Buddhist temples when Buddhism was introduced to them in the first century A.D., but the Chinese arranged the flowers in massive bronze ceremonial vessels. These early priests felt it was improper to place flowers carelessly on the altar before Buddha, so they created symbolic arrangements.

The early Buddhist temple art form is called *Shin-o-hana* and has become the basis for all Oriental floral design principles. The Chinese floral designers created their flower arrangements to suit the seasons, varying the styles according to the plant materials available. The arrangements were usually large and symmetrical, with only one or two types of foliage and flowers being placed around a central branch or main axis. Bright colors were favored in these designs, with the color of the flowers contrasting with the urn used to support them. The flowers having the lightest colors were used at the outer portions of the design and darker colors were kept nearest to the base.

The Japanese Style

The art of Japanese flower arrangement can be traced to the Asuka period during the sixth century. During this period, the Japanese adopted the Chinese language, writing methods, and Buddhist religion into their culture. Buddhism was originated in Japan about A.D. 592 by Prince Umayada, a regent of the Japanese Empress Suiko. Under his direction, special envoys were sent to China to collect knowledge of the culture and to receive instruction in the Buddhist religion. The Chinese culture was currently at a peak in its political and artistic development, so the Japanese envoys brought with them a wealth of cultural changes and new dimensions to their Japanese homeland. Among the many arts founded in Japan following this cultural revolution was an appreciation for the temple floral arrangement skills used by the Buddhist priests of China.

The successor to Prince Umayada as regent of Japan was Ono-no-Imoko. At the conclusion of his political career, he became a Buddhist priest and adopted a secluded life-style. He took the name of Ike-no-bo, which means "Hermit-by-the-lake." Ike-no-bo spent his life in meditation and in the arrangement of flowers for Buddhist ceremonies. Because of his refinement of the art and ritual of flower arrangement for Japanese Buddhist temple altars, his instruction was sought by other Buddhist priests.

He is credited with having established the first Japanese school of floral art in Japan, which bears his priestly name—*Ikenobo*.

The Ikenobo school of Japanese floral arrangement is still in existence today. Many other schools of flower arrangement have evolved from this original one, each one differing slightly in the philosophy of the school's grand master, in styles and freedom of expression, and in the terminology used to describe the floral design elements. Although these differences are present within the Japanese floral arts, the basic principles may be traced back to the teachings of the Ikenobo school.

The art of Japanese flower arranging has evolved through various periods since its beginning in the Ikenobo school. The basic Japanese floral design styles are Ikenobo, Rikkwa, Shokwa, Nageire, Moribana, and Jiyu-Bana.

Ikenobo: This arrangement style became the basis for later development of the floral arts in Japan. The principles of this style have been continuously used since its inception in the seventh century. The name of Ikenobo has since been popularized to *Ikebana*—"giving life to flowers," which is generally interpreted as the art of Japanese floral arrangement.

Rikkwa: This is the formal temple style of Japanese flower arrangements. It evolved from the basic Chinese temple art style known as Shin-o-hana, as it was refined by Ike-no-bo in seventh-century Japan. This style is characterized by the massive, symmetrical arrangement of plant materials placed in a bronze ceremonial vase. These arrangements depict scenes of nature that may reach to a height of fifteen feet and require several days to complete. Symmetry of design is emphasized and the plant materials are arranged stiffly and upright in the ceremonial vase in a pyramidal form.

The first written rules of Japanese floral arrangement were made in A.D. 1039 by Senkei, a Japanese flower master of the Ikenobo school. These rules applied to the Rikkwa style of arrangement through depicting natural scenes. The rules utilized three main structural elements in each design:

Shin   The principal line of the arrangement. This element represents the *distant view* and is most often depicted by use of trees in the background.

Soe   (or Nagashi) The secondary line of the arrangement. This element represents the *middle view* and is depicted by use of low shrubbery placed in front of the trees.

Tai   (or Uke) The tertiary line of the arrangement. This element represents the *close view* and is depicted by use of small flowers in the foreground of the design.

In addition to the three main structural elements of the Japanese arrangement, helper flowers (plants) or fillers, called *Nejime* (or *Jushi*), are often added to complete the designs. Each structural element is placed in the design in strict relationship to the others and to the container in regard to their angle and height. Through the development of the Rikkwa style, Japanese flower arrangements evolved into three-dimensional designs that were later adapted into Western floral arrangements.

Shokwa (or Seika): By the middle of the fifteenth century, the Ikenobo floral styles had become less formal and rigid in their structure. The Shokwa floral arrangement style was first created by the Buddhist priest and floral master known as Senchin, of the Ikenobo school. This design style is now known as the Ikenobo Classical style of Japanese design.

Senchin began creating floral arrangements in low, flat containers— a definite break from the traditional Rikkwa styles. The name Shokwa means "quiet flowers" which is shown by the more informal presentation of these floral designs. Senchin also introduced the asymmetrically balanced style to Japanese flower arrangements. The three main structural elements of Shin-Soe-Tai were changed to represent: heaven = Shin, man = Soe, and earth = Tai. This principle of three is interpreted to show that "man is found between the sphere of heaven and the soil of the earth." These elements have continued to be used throughout Japanese floral design history. By using these main elements and their modifiers or filler flowers, more creative designs could be adapted to use in Japanese homes for their tea ceremonies on a smaller scale than the traditional designs of the Rikkwa style.

Nageire: At the same time as the Shokwa style was being adapted into the Japanese floral art, another informal style of design was emerging. The floral master, Enshu Kobori, began the development of floral arrangements having curving lines, rather than the more rigid triangular shapes. His use of curving branches and shapes was readily adaptable to everyday use and became popular for occasions other than the religious tea ceremony.

One of the prominent styles that emerged from this transition in Japanese floral design in the sixteenth century was the style called Nageire (pronounced Na-geh-ee-reh). The name literally means "thrown-in." This style utilized upright vases for the containers and designs were constructed with curving lines and shapes by use of curved plant stems. The designs form a definite pattern such that a line drawn through it from each major stem element will create a triangle. Nageire arrangements are designed to be viewed from *above* the eye level, while the traditional Shokwa design is to be viewed *at* eye level. Although this is called the *vase-style* design, arrangements are often created in hanging containers and other styles of vases.

Moribana: The Moribana (pronounced Mor-ee-bah-na) style of flower arrangement was originated by Unshin Ohara, a floral master of the Ike-nobo school, in the 1890s. The term moribana means "piled-up flowers," yet these designs are graceful in their simplicity and naturalness. This style has become the traditional floral style for twentieth-century Japanese arrangements.

The Moribana style uses a naturalness in arrangements that is not found in the more formal styles of past periods of Japanese floral design. This is an informal, graceful floral style that is created through the use of imagination and asymmetry. Low, flat containers are used to create replicas of the dish gardens used by the ancient Chinese. Instead of using plants in soil, however, cut blooms and plant materials are placed together to create the miniature gardens in containers. This style is based upon the triadic structural form (principle of three) adopted from the Rikkwa style — the principal elements of Shin-Soe-Tai. This floral design style was created during a general movement away from religious symbolism in flower arrangements, so it is intended to be viewed from *below* eye level, such as on a low table in the home.

Jiyu-Bana: This design style is called the *free-style* form of Japanese flower arrangement. It evolved following the end of World War II, when the Japanese adopted the culture from the Western world. These designs emphasize the form and texture of the plant material rather than interpret scenes in nature. The free-style Japanese modern designs are most closely associated with the *modern interpretive* arrangements created in America and western Europe today (Figure 1–5).

FIGURE 1–5
A modern interpretive design using anthurium, croton leaves, and contorted filbert twigs.

GUIDELINES FOR JAPANESE FLOWER ARRANGEMENT

Many Japanese flower arrangement schools have evolved over the centuries. Since each school has established its own set of rules and fundamental styles of design, it is difficult to present the many variations that are used. Therefore, descriptions outlined by the Ichiyo School of Japan are presented for two important design systems, Nageire and Moribana.

Nageire (Slanting style)

Main Stem (Shin): The main stem length is determined as one-half of the container diameter plus the container height. (Example: container diameter = 3 in., container height = 7 in.; the main stem length = (3 in. + 7 in.)/2 = 5 in.) Because this stem height extends above the top of the container, enough extra stem must be included to place it into the water and also for anchorage.

The main stem is placed at a 50-degree slant from the vertical center line and toward the left side and one-third the distance from the edge of the container.

Secondary Stem (Soe): The secondary stem is placed in the same position as the main stem, but is given only a 30-degree slant toward the center and front of the container. The height of the secondary stem is three-fourths that of the main stem (Shin).

Tertiary Stem (Tai): The tertiary stem has a height of only three-fourths that of the secondary stem. It is placed with a 70-degree slant toward the front and side opposite the main stem.

Moribana (Flat Style)

Main Stem (Shin): The main stem should be shorter than the container width. It is placed to the side of the first needlepoint holder (Kenzan), with a 25-degree slant toward the center and front from the central vertical axis.

Secondary Stem (Soe): The height of the secondary stem is three-fourths that of the main stem. It is placed at the back of the same Kenzan as the main stem and is positioned vertically along the central axis of the design.

Tertiary Stem (Tai): The height of Tai is three-fourths that of Soe. It is supported by its own Kenzan placed to the front of the container. The tertiary stem is then placed to the front of the second Kenzan with a 45-degree slant to the front.

Moribana (Upright Style)

Main Stem (Shin): The height of the main stem for an upright Moribana arrangement is one and one-half times the diameter plus the height of the container. This stem is placed in a vertical position at the rear of the Kenzan, with a 5-degree slant toward the front of the container.

Secondary Stem (Soe): The height of Soe is three-fourths that of Shin. It is placed to the side of the Kenzan at a 25-degree slant toward the center and front.

Tertiary Stem (Tai): The height of the tertiary stem is three-fourths that of the secondary stem. It is located at the front of the Kenzan and given a 45-degree slant toward the front of the container and the opposite side from the secondary stem.

Some common rules of Japanese design

1. The *line* of the arrangement is emphasized without regard to color or mass of the design. Most arrangements will have an asymmetrical triangular outline from the tips of the three stem elements.
2. *Simplicity* is regarded as most important to the fundamental principles of Japanese design. Each stem or flower is groomed for its best appearance. Filler or helper flowers are included to strengthen the line of the design. They are always placed sparingly along the axis of the stem element they are to assist and are always shorter than this stem.
3. Each flower, leaf, and stem tip is arranged to face the viewer and the stems are angled upward to appear still growing.
4. Containers are selected carefully to enhance and complement the Japanese design. These are generally formed from bronze, brass, silver, pottery, or bamboo. The Moribana arrangement requires a low, footed bowl. The Nageire designs call for an upright vase or hanging flower container of Japanese design. A large urn may be used for the heavy stems called for in the Shokwa tradition.

CONTEMPORARY AMERICAN FLOWER ARRANGEMENTS

The ending of the Victorian design era was brought about by World War I, the emancipation of women, and a desire to return to a less expensive, informal life-style by the American people. The artistic styles of the American flower arrangements changed little during the early part of the twentieth century. These either were copied from preceding periods or, more often, were blends of several design styles. The corsage became a popular floral piece during the 1920s to be worn for special occasions, especially at weddings. This custom has survived and modern corsages are well designed and functional.

The renewed interest in the Japanese culture following the end of World War II brought about some major changes in the American floral arts. While the floral design styles of continental Europe have continued the tradition of loosely arranged mass designs, American flower arrangements have incorporated the *line-mass* style. The new art movement of the early century in Europe placed an emphasis on rhythm in design, more pleasing color schemes, and more natural appearance in massed arrangements. The modern American flower arrangement is the result of the blending of this new art concept with the formal line design of the Orient. These flower arrangements are an individual expression of the artist, yet their creation requires a thorough knowledge of the art principles, elements, and construction techniques.

SELECTED REFERENCES

CONWAY, F. G. *Conway's Encyclopedia of Flower Arrangement*. New York: Alfred A. Knopf, 1970.

FORT, V. P. *A Complete Guide to Flower Arrangement*. New York: Viking Press, 1962.

HAWKES, F. A. *The Gracious Art of Flower Arrangement*. Garden City, N.Y.: Doubleday & Company, Inc., 1969.

ROCKWELL, F. F., and E. C. GRAYSON. *The Rockwells' New Complete Book of Flower Arrangement*. Garden City, N.Y.: Doubleday & Company, Inc., 1960.

TERMS TO KNOW

Ikenobo	Line design	Moribana	Rikkwa	Shokwa
Jiyu-Bana	Line-mass design	Nageire	Rococo	Soe
Liknon	Mass design	Nejime	Shin	Tai

STUDY QUESTIONS

1. Explain how the painters and artists of the Renaissance period helped to establish the floral design trends in Europe. What was the purpose of these flower arrangements used by the artists?
2. Explain why large, brightly colored, massed arrangements were popular during the sixteenth to nineteenth centuries in Europe.
3. Explain how the Oriental and European floral design styles have influenced the types of flower shop arrangements sold today.
4. Discuss why floral design styles often changed with the rise to power of various European rulers.
5. Explain how the development of plant breeding as a science may have influenced the art of flower arranging.

SUGGESTED ACTIVITIES

1. Make a poster-board display of various flower arrangement styles from earlier periods of history. Identify the period (approximate) and tell why you think this is correct. The class can obtain pictures from magazines and arrange them on the poster board.
2. Visit an art gallery or museum to observe the floral designs that depict earlier periods of history.
3. Select specific flower arrangement pictures from magazines and have a class discussion about the use of flowers in the designs. Explain what makes them either masculine or feminine in emotion. How does the container influence the style of the design?

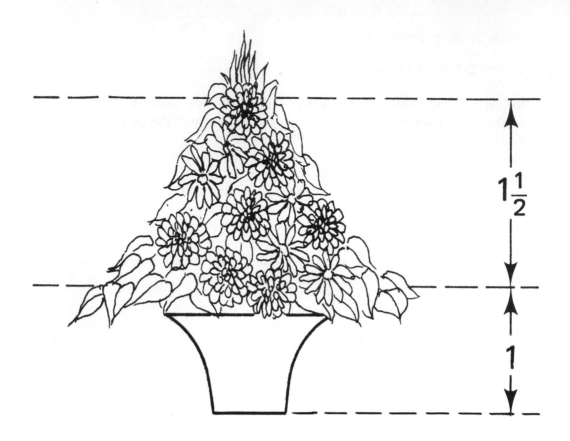

$1\frac{1}{2}$

1

CHAPTER 2:

The Principles and Elements of Floral Design

As with other artistic media, flowers are arranged by designers according to established guidelines. These govern the placement of flowers in a container in a manner similar to the creation of a painting or sculpture. Although flowers will not always allow the designer to adhere strictly to these design guides, the beginning flower arranger should acquire a working knowledge of them early in training. Once these design principles and elements are well understood, more freedom of expression and creativity will be possible for the floral designer.

THE PRINCIPLES OF DESIGN

Different floral art authorities use various terminology to describe the principles of design for flower arranging. The basic terminology for the principles discussed here are the most widely accepted and should be used by student designers whenever discussing or evaluating flower arrangements. In all arrangements, the floral designer is striving for emphasis, balance, proportion, rhythm, harmony, and unity.

Emphasis

Emphasis is achieved in a floral design by creating an accented area or a *focal point*. The focal point is the area of an arrangement that will draw the most attention and will direct the eye of a viewer to a specific location within the design. The accented area of most conventional florists' designs is located immediately in front of and slightly above the rim of the floral container. This area will be at the geometric center of a well-balanced design.

The purpose of the focal flowers is to visually draw all of the elements of the design to a single location, the *center of interest*. An accent will exist whenever contrast is present in a design. This contrast may be in the form of flower sizes, colors, textures, or shapes. The most striking contrast in a design is created by use of brightly colored flowers at the center of interest with less vibrant tones or tints used as the flowers approach the outer perimeters of the design. A designer will purposely space flowers far apart at the perimeters of an arrangement and closer together near the focal area. The flowers, however, should never be crowded to form a tightened mass of blooms. Generally, it will not be necessary to allow individual blooms to touch each other; rather, to allow them to appear loose and natural, with some foliage protruding between the petals.

Accents can be created in a floral design by the proper selection of flower types and color combinations. In traditional flower arrangements, a graduation in flower sizes is used to create emphasis. Large flower types and those that have opened most create an accent because of their size. Emphasis can most easily be achieved in a design when the smallest, least-open flowers are placed at the perimeter of the arrangement and the large, fully developed flowers are located at the focal point.

Flowers with unique shapes also attract attention. These can be used to create a satisfactory accent at the focal point of an arrangement. Often a single unique flower will create an accent, but usually a floral designer will use three of these flowers to emphasize a large arrangement.

Another striking contrast may be created by using varying degrees of flower and foliage textures within an arrangement. Coarser textures will appear to have more visual weight, so they will be best used at the focal point. An accessory, such as a ribbon or bow, is often used by retail florists to create emphasis in bouquets and corsages. The contrast in texture or color will place the emphasis at the lip of the container. Some floral design styles will not require an accent area. The mass-design styles of early American and European history were created without the placement of a focal point. When recreating these designs, no center of interest should be present.

Balance

A well-designed arrangement will appear to be stable and self-supporting. An arrangement should possess both mechanical and visual balance. Mechanical balance is achieved when the container is the proper size and weight for the size of flowers being used with it. The design

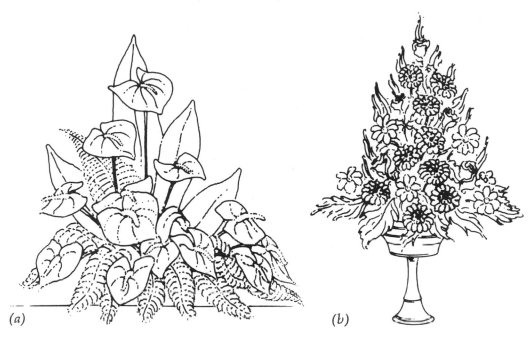

(a) (b)

FIGURE 2–1 Balance in design. (a) Asymmetrical balance. (b) Symmetrical balance.

should have the flowers distributed properly so that the container will support them. This is accomplished by the convergence of lines at the focal point. The flower and foliage stems should appear to arise from a single central location in the container. Balance is lost when the arrangement can be divided into several parts or areas.

An arrangement may be composed of symmetrical or asymmetrical balance (see Figure 2–1). A symmetrical design will appear to be the same on each side of a vertical center line. A formal balance is created when the focal point is centered in the container. Many floral design styles are arranged with asymmetrical balance. This gives the appearance of a more natural design and allows the arranger more originality in his or her work. Visual balance must be carefully planned for when the asymmetrical design is created. The size relationship of flower stems, distance from the focal point, and color density must be considered in this type of balance. The asymmetrical design will have a high side and a low side divided by the focal area. The height-to-width relationship of these designs must allow the arrangements to maintain their stability.

Flowers are arranged from the back of the container toward the front and sides. Depth and visual balance are created in the design when the rear flower stems tip backward slightly and the focal flower is placed well in front of the lip of the container. Flower heights are gradually lowered as each flower is placed closer to the front of the arrangement. Balance is maintained by grading flowers by color, texture, size, and spacing. This gives the arrangement a feeling of depth and support.

Proportion

A floral arrangement appears best when all the component flowers are related in size, color, texture, and shape. The scale of a design is dictated by the size of arrangement and its relationship to its surroundings. A small centerpiece placed on the stage of a large auditorium would be lost from the audience's view. This same relationship may be applied to the flowers placed within the design. Proportion in an arrangement is accomplished by scaling flowers toward the focal point. This means that the smallest buds are placed farthest from the visual center of the design. The flowers are then graduated in size by the placement of increasingly larger flowers in the arrangement until the center of interest is reached. Here are placed the largest or showiest flowers in the design.

The use of *negative spaces* or voids within the arrangement is equally as important as sizes of flowers in creating a pleasing proportion. Flowers placed at the same heights within the design will fight for equal attention. Spaces without flowers are purposely left to allow each bloom to be viewed singly. An example of the use of negative space in design is shown by the curvilinear arrangement styles described in Chapter 4. Here, a visual line is left incompleted with the void balanced by flowers to create the curved line of the design (see Figure 2–2). The absence of flowers in these areas adds interest and proportion within the design.

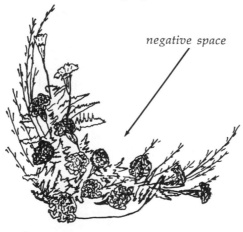

negative space

FIGURE 2–2
The crescent design shows
the effective use of negative space
in creating asymmetrical balance.

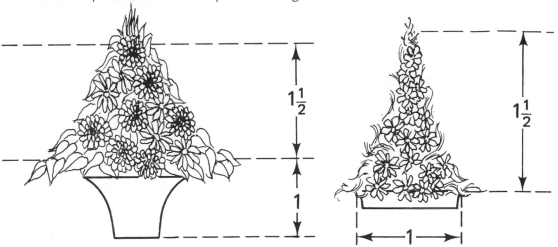

FIGURE 2–3   *Height of an arrangement. The overall height of an arrangement is generally 1½ times the height or width of the container.*

Good proportion in an arrangement is created by establishing a pleasing scale relationship of the flowers to the container. A generally accepted rule of floral design states that for a tall container, plant material should be at least one and one-half to two times the height of the vase. For low, flat containers the height of an arrangement is at least one and one-half to two times the width (see Figure 2–3). This rule is not iron-clad and may be altered provided that good proportion in the design is maintained.

An arrangement that would exceed these height limitations would be one where very visually lightweight foliage and flowers are used. Balance and proportion are easily maintained in a tall, delicate-appearing design. A horizontal-style design will have its primary axis running along its width. The height of this type of design would be drastically reduced from the designated rules. The beginning floral designer should use these height relationships as a guide, however, until more design experience has been gained and variations in styles are desired.

Proportion or scale must be carefully controlled as the designer selects the flowers and locates them in the arrangement. For example, using large orchids with tiny violets will appear out of proportion. This will be apparent because a drastic contrast in size and texture of the flowers exists. However, a monotonous design would be created with the use of flowers of exactly the same size, color, and texture throughout the arrangement.

Rhythm

As a floral arrangement is seen and experienced the viewer should be able to take in all parts of its design, yet should continuously be led back to the focal point or visual center of interest. This visual movement is created by the rhythm of the design. Rhythm is the apparent flow of lines, textures, or colors that express a feeling of motion rather than confusion in an arrangement. Motion is created most easily in a design having a curved line. Here the viewer is attracted gently from the top of the arrangement, along the curving elements of line or texture or color through to its focal point, the center of interest. Rhythm may be achieved in several ways —through *opposition, repetition, radiation,* or *transition.*

When flowers having the same color, texture, or form are placed at opposing points away from the focal point, the center of interest is emphasized. These opposing flowers create a balance in the design that naturally leads the eye from one point, through the focal area, and on to the other side of the design. This eye movement is the cause for the visual motion within the design.

The repetition of the same flower types throughout an arrangement ties all of the parts into a single unit. The viewer will see the entire design through a repeated use of the same colors, textures, or flower shapes. When flowers are placed with their stems originating at the focal point, they will appear to radiate from the center of the design. This radiation from a single point will create an emphasis at the center of interest and a visual movement is provided.

A transition in color and texture or the gradation of scaled flower sizes can also be used to create motion in a design. The darkest or brightest color may be placed at the focal point. From the center to the outer edges of the arrangement, the intensity or tone of the color is graded to be more subdued. A similar use of textural-quality transition will be effective in creating motion within the design that leads the eye to the center of interest in the arrangement.

Harmony

When an arrangement possesses harmony, all of the design parts will fit together into a pleasing composition of flower shapes, colors, textures, and sizes. This could be interpreted to mean that the idea or theme of the design has been successfully created. In order for harmony to be achieved, all of the component parts of the design must be combined in an appealing relationship.

Unity

Unity is created when all of the design parts blend together without a noticeable separation. Although each flower or area of the arrangement may be distinctive, all elements must visually blend together. Unity is best achieved by repeating related flower types, colors, and textures throughout the design. This helps to pull the components together with the focal point as the center of interest. When one color or type of flower is used only at the perimeter of the arrangement and another at the center, no unity will be felt by the viewer of the design (see Figure 2–4).

FIGURE 2–4 *Lack of unity. Unity is lacking when the arrangement can be divided into separate parts.*

THE DESIGN ELEMENTS

The principles of design are used to create a successful flower arrangement. The elements of good design are used in achieving those principles, much like building blocks are used to make a structure. The principles of design are similar to a recipe with the elements of design as the ingredients. In order to create successful flower arrangements through the use of the design principles, the following design elements must be understood: line, form, texture, and color.

Line

Line in a flower arrangement is the visual path that the eye travels as it passes through the arrangement. The line establishes the skeleton of the design, particularly when linear flowers or foliages are used. This element produces the underlying framework of the arrangement that holds the composition together. The line of an arrangement may also be created by repetition of similar flower colors, textures, or shapes.

Certain emotional qualities are evident in the line of an arrangement. A vertical line gives the arrangement an appearance of strength. A curved line adds gentleness or gracefulness and gives the impression of motion. A horizontal line is more relaxing or informal, so is used most often for table arrangements.

Form

The flowers, foliages, and containers used in flower arrangements have various shapes or forms. Flower and foliage shapes add a visual quality that is important in developing harmony, creating rhythm, and establishing a focal point. Form is also expressed by the geometric shape that creates the outline of the design. This concept of the design elements will be discussed in further detail in Chapter 4.

Texture

Texture refers to such surface qualities of flowers and foliage as smoothness, glossiness, and roughness. This quality of texture may be expressed either as a physical or a visual characteristic of the plant material. For example, it may be used to describe leaf or stem patterns. Fine-textured flowers or leaves are located at the farthest points from the center of interest in the design. The focal point of the arrangement will create emphasis when coarse-textured flowers are placed in this area. Contrasts between coarse and fine textures will provide a dramatic accent in an arrangement. However, this contrast of textural qualities is successful only when a balance of the two extremes exists. The texture of each part of an arrangement should blend pleasingly together to maintain unity within the design.

COLOR IN FLORAL DESIGN

The fourth element of the floral design principles is *color*. The correct use of color in creating a well-designed flower arrangement is so important that it is given special emphasis in this chapter. The design principles cannot function properly within an arrangement unless the flower colors are carefully blended and positioned in a pleasing composition. The color of the individual flowers used in an arrangement will affect the mood of the design as it relates to the setting within a room, the message that it conveys, and the success of the designer in creating an attractive arrangement.

A discussion of color theory must be understood before flowers may be used properly in a flower arrangement. Unlike paints, flower colors are derived from the chemical pigments found within the petals, leaves, and stems. Petal pigments may be derived from chemicals which reflect either as white, green, red, yellow, or blue. The combination of these pigments in the petal cells will determine the color as it is perceived. For example, when a flower petal contains a large quantity of white pigment and only a small amount of red, the resulting petal color will be pink. Although flower colors are not always present in their pure form, generally being mixtures of two or more colors in their petals and foliage, the designer must be able to mix these flower colors in a manner that will impart a pleasing relationship to the viewer.

The Color Wheel

Colors are perceived as a visual response to light as it is separated into individual wavelengths. As light passes through moisture in the atmosphere or a glass prism, the color pattern that results is a rainbow band of the spectrum colors. Close inspection of the color spectrum shows that twelve major colors are present: red, red-orange, orange, yellow-orange, yellow, yellow-green, green, blue-green, blue, blue-violet, violet, and red-violet.

The pigments used in the creation of colors form the basis for color theory in design. The *color wheel* is a useful tool in studying these pigments and their relationships in forming successful color harmonies in floral design (see Figure 2–5). The following terminology is used to describe the color characteristics of pigments in color theory:

Primary colors: In pigment theory, the primary colors form the basis from which all other colors may be derived. These are called the primary colors because they cannot be created by mixing any other colors. The primary colors of a color wheel are red, yellow, and blue. Mixing all three primary colors in equal amounts will create a black pigment.

Secondary colors: Whenever two primary colors are mixed in equal proportions, the resulting mixture becomes a secondary color. The combination of primary colors in this manner provides a pleasing color harmony and is often found in the petals of flowers. The secondary colors are: *green, violet,* and *orange.*

Tertiary colors: Equal mixing of a primary color with an adjacent secondary pigment color results in the creation of a tertiary color. These carry the name of both colors that are used with the primary color named first. For example, yellow plus orange creates the tertiary color of yellow-orange. The tertiary colors of a color wheel are red-orange, yellow-orange, yellow-green, blue-green, blue-violet, and red-violet.

Colors have other characteristics that are important in the arrangement of flowers. The following terms are used to describe colors: hue, value, intensity, tint, shade, and tone.

Hue: This term is a synonym for color. It is used to differentiate one color from another. The twelve colors on the color wheel at their fullest brilliance are the basic hues of color in design. Any color variation that results from dilution with white, black, or gray is still related to the basic hue within a color family.

Value: A hue will exhibit various degrees of value, depending upon the amount of black or white that is added. This term describes the lightness or darkness of a hue. Degrees of lightness or darkness of a hue are called *tints* or *shades.*

Tint: When any hue is mixed with white pigment, it is lightened. These tints are called high or light values and produce the pastels of a hue. The tint of the red hue is pink, which is produced by lightening red with white pigment. The tints of a hue add restfulness and impart a delicate contrast to an arrangement. When tints are used in a flower arrangement, the lightness of the flower colors will soften the darker hues. Flowers having the lightened values will appear daintier and will provide an uplifting effect in the design.

Shades: When black is added to a color, it is darkened, and a shade of the hue is created. These are called the lower or darker values of a hue.

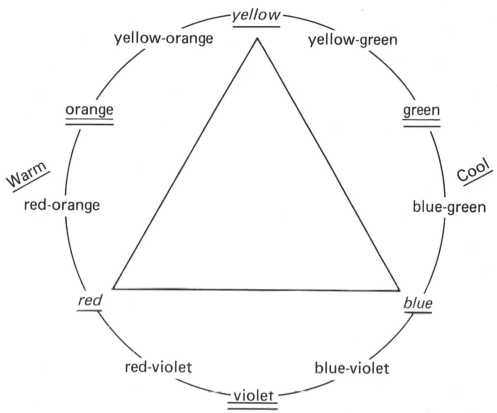

FIGURE 2–5 *The color wheel can be used as an aid to the designer in developing pleasing color schemes.*

The shade of the red hue is maroon. When shades of a hue are used together with tints, the shades will appear heaviest. Flowers having the darker values should be used nearest the focal point to lend stability to an arrangement. Arrangements composed of either the tints or shades of hues alone will appear monotonous or motionless. Adding flower color tints to a design having color shades will reduce the depressing effect often felt when color shades are used alone.

Intensity: A flower color possesses an intensity. This is a visual quality of brightness or dullness created by adding different amounts of gray. Intensity is a measure of the brilliance or purity of a hue. When a hue is at its greatest intensity, it is said to be at its fullest *chroma*. This is the strongest quality that the hue may attain, because it is not diluted with white, black, or gray. In flowers, the color intensity is determined by the relative quantity of pigment present in the cells.

Tone: This is a measure of the color intensity when the hue is diluted by gray. Adding both black and white to any spectrum hue will reduce the brilliance of the color. The amount of gray added may vary until the hue is reduced to a very dull appearing intensity. The tonal qualities of flower colors may be neutralized in much the same manner by use of equal amounts of colors lying exactly opposite on the color wheel (direct complementary colors).

Neutral colors

The pigment colors of black, white, and the grays, which result from mixing black and white, make up the neutral colors. These colors are so reduced in value and intensity that they no longer possess any identifiable chroma colors. Flower color is translucent, rather than being opaque as with pigments. When a flower appears as having a white coloration, it is because all light wavelengths are being *reflected* to the eyes. The combination of all colors being reflected means that the white petals possess *no* color at all. Because white cannot be identified with any particular hue family on the color wheel, it will blend perfectly with any color grouping. However, because white is so brilliant, care must be taken in both quantity and placement of white flowers in arrangements. White containers are best used only for arrangements containing large amounts of pastels and those having a daintier appearance. The strong contrast between a white container and darker shades or dull tones of flower hues could produce an undesirable accent at the container rather than at the focal area of a design.

Black and gray create heaviness in an arrangement and must be used sparingly. Black is the opposite of white in that black *absorbs* all light wavelengths. This results in black objects containing all of the spectrum colors. Using black in an arrangement is not a problem for the student of floral design, since no truly black flowers may be found. Those that appear black are actually the deeper shades of blue or violet. When hues of blue, red, or violet are used with these flower color types, the resulting blend brings out the true blue or violet contrasts. Black should be used only for containers or in accessories that accompany a design. The container having a black or gray color will provide a balanced visual strength and stability to a design. Occasionally the designer may wish to add a touch of black or gray to the foliage in a design by use of color dyes or spray paint. Whenever this is done, only small quantities of black should be used which requires balancing by greater amounts of other selected hues.

Emotional Qualities of Color

Colors are used in arrangements for creating emotional impressions. Color may influence a psychological response through the design by imparting such emotions as warmth, coolness, joy, love, sympathy, or it may suggest a seasonal message when used with the correct flowers. Certain spectrum colors will dominate others when used in a floral composition. The degree to which the colors add drama or restfulness is called the visual quality of warmth or coolness.

Warm colors are those containing either yellow, red, or orange hues. These are associated with warmth because they are the colors of fire, sun, and heat. The warm colors appear to move toward the viewer or dominate a composition, so they are called *advancing* colors (xanthic colors). These colors may be used to create a dramatic impact in a design. They appear best when used in full sunlight, dim light, or under incandescent lighting.

Cool colors (cyanic colors) have a *receding* visual effect when used in an arrangement. They give the impression of fading into the background or moving away from the viewer. They suggest the coolness of shade, sky, or grass. The cool colors of green, blue, and violet will reduce the tonal qualities of warm-colored flowers when they are used together. Arrangements having blue or violet as the dominant colors should not be used for display in a large auditorium, since these colors are lost from view at a distance. Under artificial lighting, particularly fluorescent lamps, the blue is muddied and may not appear true to its color or intensity. Under daylight or candlelight, the cool colors are more vibrant.

Violet-colored flowers may be used successfully in either a warm or a cool color scheme, because this hue is composed of mixtures of both red and blue. When violet is used beside red, the red in the violet dominates and the blue recedes from view. The opposite is true when violet-colored flowers are used together with blue in a design. Flowers having cool-colored petals will not provide as much drama as will those having warm-colored petals. When this contrast or dramatic effect is required, more cool-colored flowers will be required in the design to provide a visual balance of color.

Symbolism of Color in Design

Each of the hues found in flower petals or foliage conveys a message to the viewer of a floral design. These color-translated messages may be used by the designer to create a theme or to command an emotional response to an arrangement.

Red gives the feeling of excitement to a design. It should be used sparingly with large quantities of other colors for balance. The spectrum hue of red is overpowering and may be lessened in its dramatic effect by the addition of its tint (pink) or shade (maroon). A restful mood is created when a design is composed of either pink or light rose hues alone. Other symbolic messages conveyed by the red hue are love (such as red carnations and roses), fire, and blood (as a symbol for martyrdom).

Orange provides radiance to an arrangement. It is not as dramatic as the other warm colors of red and yellow, but is tempered by being a mixture of both hues. More pleasing hues of orange are its tints and shades (peach, melon, brown). These are often used in autumn arrangements where natural fall foliage colors are popular.

Yellow is said to be the most versatile of all the spectrum colors. It may add a dramatic effect to a design when used at its fullest intensity. More often it is found in flower colors as a tint, that is, softened by white, or as a shade having a golden tone. This color will always add spirit to an otherwise dull-appearing design. Yellow flowers are selected often for use in springtime designs and for weddings. Yellow also symbolizes cheerfulness, sun, and wealth.

Green is a color that is found in the foliage and stems of most flowers. It has a softening effect on the lighter flower petals because it belongs to the class of cool colors. It provides an excellent background for arrangements and is a color of choice for containers that will not attract unwanted attention.

Blue may add darkness to an arrangement. Being a receding color, it softens the color scheme of an arrangement. When used with warm colors of red or yellow, it becomes subordinated. Blue flowers suggest the peacefulness of water and solitude. It is a good color to use for dinner table arrangements where an intimate atmosphere is desired. Blue is considered a masculine color and is often preferred by men. It is intensified when used with brown, silver, or gold.

Violet borders both the warm and cool colors on the color wheel. When violet is used with blue, it takes on the restfulness of a receding color. When used with red, the vibrancy of the warm color is emphasized. Violet or purple is associated with royalty and is often found in arrangements used for religious purposes. Violet-colored flowers are most attractive when combined with yellow or gold. Brown provides an excellent background for violet-colored flowers.

Color Schemes in Floral Design

A pleasing combination of colors is desired in all flower arrangements. The use of different color combinations within an arrangement can change the entire mood and character of the design. The flower and foliage colors are combined in a floral arrangement to create pleasing color schemes. The most common color schemes used by florists when designing are accented neutral, monochromatic, analogous, complementary, split-complementary, and the triad.

Accented Neutral: The accented neutral color scheme is composed of flowers having any of the various hues used alone with a neutral background. A single accent color is selected for emphasis. The background flowers and foliage may be white, gray, or black (often obtained with floral tints or paints). The hues of tan and brown are also sometimes used in this color scheme. This color scheme finds its greatest use in a room decoration where the wall covering or drapery is heavily patterned. The presence of an arrangement having several colors that repeat those in the pattern would be lost or fade into the background. By selecting only a single color from the wall or drapery pattern and accenting it against neutral-colored flowers, the arrangement will become a dominant feature in the room. The neutral color that is most often selected for use in floral designs is white because it is frequently found in flowers.

Monochromatic: A monochromatic color scheme is created from flowers and foliages having the tints and shades of a single hue. It is another color scheme that can be used safely in a room where many other colors are already present. A single color may be emphasized in a monochromatic design to add drama to the room decor. This color scheme features a single hue of the spectrum with a full range of its value and intensity being utilized. An example of a monochromatic color scheme featuring the tints and shades of red-orange is shown in the accompanying chart.

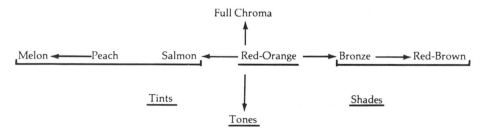

A truly monochromatic design must be composed of flowers, foliage, and a container all related to only one hue. Flower petals often cannot be found in only a single hue. When a flower color is a single color, the stamens or throat are often composed of another color. Furthermore, plant foliage is more than likely green, as are the customary florists' foliages used in arranging. The floral designer should learn to select floral material having the most exacting colors to fit the monochromatic scheme when such material is available. However, the designer should be concerned only with the overall effect of color in this color scheme. The green foliage will be used in such a small amount that it will not detract from the intended color scheme. Slight variations in stamen or throat colors will likewise not be serious. The monochromatic color scheme is usually composed from flowers having either yellow, yellow-green, yellow-orange, orange, red-orange, or red petals because these may most easily be duplicated in both flowers and foliages at various periods of the year.

When constructing a monochromatic color scheme, it is very important that color unity exists throughout the design. The lighter hues (tints) should be used high and at the perimeters of the design to add lightness. The darker hues (shades) will add weight, so they must be used nearest to the focal point. Unity is provided only when a balance is achieved among the values of the hue. Intermediates in color value may be used between the outer perimeter flowers (tints) and the focal flowers (shades). Some of the darker-hued flowers should be carried into the outer perimeter of the design. Being visually heavy, they must be spaced far apart and used sparingly. The lighter tints should be located within the darker hues at the focal area for the same reason. The overall impression should be that the lighter values of flowers are carried throughout the design and those having the darker values are also. The designer must avoid separating the arrangement into zones with a single color value.

Analogous: An analogous color scheme is created by combining any three hues found next to each other on the color wheel. This color scheme has a great emotional appeal because any three colors that lie next to each other on the color wheel were developed from a single primary color. It is not necessary to include the primary color as part of the analogous color scheme because the secondary and tertiary colors will blend satisfactorily. The most common analogous color scheme used by florists includes the hues of yellow, yellow-green, and green. This is primarily done because green stems and foliage became an integral part of the color scheme.

Flower petals will often combine analogous colors on the same flower. The designer should learn to select flowers that will harmonize with the pattern of colors dictated by these petals. When selecting the

colors for this style of design, a single hue should be chosen to be emphasized. Intermediates between the other hues, or their tints or shades, should
then be selected to act as a background. The predominant hue will create the
emphasis while blending with its analogous colors in the design. This
color scheme is the most used in design because it is the most pleasing
and, depending on the combination of colors used, can fit harmoniously
into nearly any room decoration.

Complementary: Another appealing combination in color schemes
is one using contrasting, or complementary, colors. Any two colors located
directly across from one another on the color wheel are complements. When
the two colors are used together in an arrangement, a complementary color
scheme is created. This color scheme provides pleasing contrasts because
the complement color supplies the missing primaries of the color wheel.
An example of this can be found in the complementary color scheme using
the hues of blue and orange. Blue is a primary color and orange is the
secondary color created by the equal mixing of yellow and red. This balance of primary colors within the complementary color scheme is maintained
when a secondary hue and a tertiary hue are combined in an arrangement.

When two complementary colors are used in a design, one will be a
warm color while the other one will be a cool color. One of these colors
will dominate the design and should be selected to create emphasis in the
arrangement. The complement color should be used in the tints and shades
or grayed intensity of the hue to reduce the contrast between the two
opposing colors. Examples of complementary colors are red and green,
yellow and violet, or blue and orange used together.

Split-complementary: The split-complementary color scheme resembles a complementary color scheme except that three hues are used. In this
color scheme, a hue located on one side of the color wheel is used with each
of the hues located on either side of its complement. This color scheme is
more attractive and is easier to construct than is the complementary color
scheme. The contrast in colors is not as great with this color scheme because the two hues used on one side of the color chart balance better with
the third, particularly when it is a warm color. A single color should be
selected for emphasis in this color scheme. It is generally the color opposite the two split-complements. Some pleasing split-complementary color
schemes in floral arrangements include blue with yellow-orange and red-
orange, yellow with blue-violet and red-violet, and red with yellow-green
and blue-green.

Triad: The triadic color scheme is composed of three hues located
equidistant on the color wheel. While this color scheme provides an interesting contrast, the designer must be careful to allow only a single hue to

provide emphasis. The triad color scheme may consist of only the three primary colors of red, yellow, and blue. These colors will clash and blend in such a manner as to be perceived as all of those found on the color wheel.

Other color combinations may be found in flower arrangements at various times. The *double split-complementary* and the *tetrad* color schemes include four colors used together in the same arrangement. The double split-complementary color scheme is composed of hues that are adjacent to both direct complements. An example of the double split-complementary color scheme would be red-orange, red-violet, blue-green, and yellow-green (where the complementary colors are red and green). The tetrad color scheme combines any four colors that are equidistant from each other on the color wheel. An example of a tetrad color scheme is yellow, blue-green, violet, and red-orange. A polychromatic color scheme may include any three or more unrelated colors. These color schemes are difficult to master for the beginning floral designer. They require great skill in color harmony to create a pleasing combination of colors and flowers, while avoiding the appearance of disarray or lack of unity within a flower arrangement. Most designs will be more successfully arranged if only three or fewer flower colors are combined.

SELECTED REFERENCES

BENZ, M. *Flowers: Geometric Form*, 3rd ed. Houston, Tex.: San Jacinto Publishing Company, 1966.

CONWAY, J. G. *Conway's Encyclopedia of Flower Arrangement*. New York: Alfred A. Knopf Publishing Company, 1970.

FORT, V. P. *A Complete Guide to Flower Arrangement*. New York: Viking Press, 1962.

HILLIER, F. B. *Basic Guide to Flower Arranging*. New York: McGraw-Hill Book Company, 1974.

PFAHL, P. B. *The Retail Florist Business*. Danville, Ill.: Interstate Printers and Publishers, Inc., 1968.

ROCKWELL, F. F., and E. C. GRAYSON. *The Rockwell's New Complete Book of Flower Arrangement*. Garden City, N.Y.: Doubleday & Company, Inc., 1960.

ROGERS, J. *Flower Arranging*. New York: Hamlyn Publishing Company, 1964.

TERMS TO KNOW

Accented neutral	Emphasis	Neutral colors	Tertiary colors
Analogous	Focal point	Primary colors	Texture
Balance	Harmony	Proportion	Tone
Chroma	Intensity	Rhythm	Triad
Color wheel	Monochromatic	Secondary colors	Unity
Complementary	Negative space	Split-complementary	Value

STUDY QUESTIONS

1. List the design *principles* and give an explanation of how each is used in a floral design.
2. Explain how each of the design *elements* is used to create the principles of design.
3. Explain why a focal point is used in most flower arrangements. List the various methods that may be used to create a focal point in an arrangement.
4. Describe the four methods that may be used to create rhythm in a design. Why is this principle so important in a design?

SUGGESTED ACTIVITIES

1. Make a color wheel to be used in creating various design color schemes. Place the twelve spectrum colors on a chart using a poster board and artists' water colors. Mix all of the various hues using only the colors of red, yellow, and blue.
2. Prepare a value chart and an intensity chart using a single color mixed with white, black, or gray pigments.
3. Select pictures of flower arrangements from magazines or florists' advertisements and discuss the way flowers were used to follow the design principles and elements.
4. Using the same pictures of flower arrangements, try to determine what the theme of each arrangement might be. Discuss how the flower colors create a specific mood in each design.
5. Prepare arrows from cardboard strips to show the various color schemes described in this chapter. The arrows may be mounted on the color wheel poster board with thumb tacks to show their relationships to the colors.

CHAPTER 3:

The Mechanics of Flower Arranging

The designer in a flower shop will have available a wide array of containers, flowers, foliages, stem-supporting materials, and various other types of supplies used for the construction of flower arrangements. Although the selection of these materials will depend upon the style of design to be constructed, having a good assortment of these supplies available and a basic understanding of their uses is very important.

The floral designer should become familiar with the preparation and care of cut flowers that are received at the flower shop. The care given to the cut flowers while they are at the shop will have a definite effect upon the life of the flowers in arrangements for the consumer. Assistant designers in flower shops are usually responsible for the initial care of the flowers and customer orders as they are received. The beginning floral designer should also be capable of selecting suitable containers, flowers, and foliage types for each of the arrangement styles created at the flower shop. A thorough knowledge of the basic stem supports and wiring methods is also necessary before the flower shop employee may begin creating the basic floral designs. These topics are discussed in detail in this chapter.

CUTTING TOOLS USED BY DESIGNERS

The floral designer will need a good-quality sharp knife for cutting the flower stems as they are being prepared for an arrangement. Most designers prefer to use their own personal knife for this purpose to avoid having to search for one every time it is needed. When cutting a flower stem, the knife is held in the hand and pulled through the stem to form a bevel cut at the base. The knife is drawn through the stem rather than

47

(a)

FIGURE 3–1   *Cutting a flower stem. (a) Hold the flower stem in one hand and hold the knife firmly in the palm of the other. (b) Pull the knife swiftly through the stem in a single motion without hitting the thumb. This method will avoid cut fingers and will make a bevel-cut stem base on the flower stem.*

(b)

being used as a saw to sever the stems (see Figure 3–1). Floral shears may be used to cut flower stems instead of using a knife. Shears that cut on both surfaces are best for use with flower stems. Shears that cut against a flat surface have a tendency to crush the flower stems. Shears with one serrated edge (sawtoothed) are required for cutting the wires used to support flower stems, wired stems of permanent flowers, and woody-stemmed materials (see Figure 3–2).

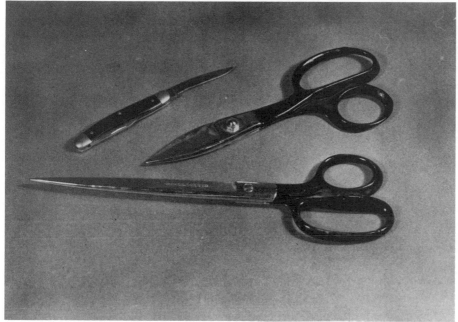

FIGURE 3–2   *The most common tools used for flower arranging: a sharp knife, ribbon scissors, and wire-cutting scissors.*

SELECTING FLOWERS AND FOLIAGE

Selecting flowers to be used in creating an arrangement is an important skill to be learned by the beginning floral designer. The designer must consider various features of the flowers when making this decision, including: (1) the seasonal availability of the flowers, (2) the colors required to fit a specified color scheme in the design, (3) the size of the finished design in relation to its placement in a room, (4) the cost of the finished arrangement, and (5) the shapes of the flowers and foliage as they influence the line and form of the arrangement.

The designer creates a style of arrangement by properly selecting those flower and foliage types that will best express the desired effect. Flower and foliage types may be classified for best use according to their shapes. The shapes of flowers and foliages used by florists are grouped into four categories: line, form, mass, and filler types.

Line Flowers and Foliages: Line flowers help to create the skeleton or outline of a design (see Figure 3–3). The typical shape of the line flower consists of a tall, erect spike of blossoms that adds height or width to an arrangement. Spike flowers that are used most often in flower arranging

FIGURE 3–3   *Some Line flowers.*

(a) *snapdragon*

(b) *larkspur*

(c) *gladiolus*

are gladiolus, snapdragons, stock, delphinium, larkspur, cattail, and various spring-flowering tree and shrub species (such as crabapple, forsythia, red-bud, and pussy willow). The line flower shape is helpful in creating the outline of the arrangement because most spikes form a gradation of flower sizes. The florets at the base of the spike are the most fully open, with a gradual progression of smaller blooms and buds toward the tip. This progression of blooms conforms to the modern line-mass style of design having the tightest buds at the perimeter of the arrangement and the fullest blooms located toward the center.

Line flowers are used in geometrical designs to define the spaces of the arrangement. The primary outline of triangular designs is created by spike flowers in forming the height and width relationship of the arrangement. These flowers are located within the body of the arrangement as well to provide unity of design. Line flowers may also be used in creating

FIGURE 3–4 *Preparing a gladiolus.*

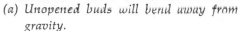

(a) *Unopened buds will bend away from gravity.*

(b) *The tip is broken off the top above the smallest bud that is slightly open.*

curvilinear designs. When creating a curve, the stems are placed in a manner that simulates a curve rather than forcing the flowers to actually bend into a curved shape.

The spike tips of the gladiolus have a tendency to bend away from gravity and point upward when placed horizontally in a design. This situation is corrected with gladiolus spikes by carefully removing a short section of the spike tip above the first floret showing some petal color. The stem of the spike tip is gently forced away from the attachment point of the last floret that is to remain on the spike (see Figure 3–4). These removed tips are saved for use in filling out the design of smaller arrangements. The gladiolus spike can be broken into smaller pieces of one or more blooms using this same technique when this practice is desirable. These smaller pieces are used throughout the body of the arrangement to create unity within the design.

FIGURE 3–5   *Some Line foliages.*

(a) Scotch broom   *(b) flat fern (Boston fern)*   *(c) spiral eucalyptus*

Foliage types having a linear shape are used to complement linear flowers in an arrangement (see Figure 3–5). The linear leaves of gladiolus and iris are incorporated into the design to reinforce the line created when these flowers are used in arrangements. The foliage from spiral eucalyptus and Scotch broom may be easily shaped to create a curvilinear line when a curve is required or they may be used to strengthen the line of any design. Some examples of line foliages used in flower arrangements are gladiolus and iris leaves, ti leaves, lycopodium, sansevieria, Scotch broom, spiral eucalyptus, and flat fern (Boston fern).

Form Flowers: Form flowers are those having distinctive shapes. These are effective as accent flowers in creating a center of interest in a geometrical design (see Figure 3–6). This flower type may be used to create a visual path for the eye to follow by pointing the blooms in one direction in a design. These flower types should be spaced adequately to provide an open appearance rather than creating a massed effect. Since these flow-

FIGURE 3–6 *Some Form flowers.*

(a) Easter lily
(b) iris

(c) calla lily
(d) anthurium

ers are generally more expensive than other flower types, they should be placed sparingly in a design. These flowers are more difficult to use properly in arrangements because their flower form will lead the eye in one direction. Skill is required to avoid a lack of harmony or disarray in the lines created when form flowers are selected. Examples of form flowers are Easter lilies, calla lilies, daylilies, anthurium, orchids, daffodils (jonquils), irises, and bird-of-paradise (Strelitzia).

FIGURE 3–6 (continued) *Two other well-known Form flowers.*

(e) Cattleya orchid   *(f) Cymbidium orchid.*

    Mass Flowers and Foliages: Mass flowers are composed of a single stem having one rounded flower head at the top (see Figure 3–7). These are excellent for adding mass to an arrangement. Larger blooms may be selected to create a focal point because they will add visual weight and balance to an arrangement. The flowers are graded in size from the top of

FIGURE 3–7 Representative Mass flowers include

the standard rose   the sweetheart rose

FIGURE 3–7 (contd)
Other Mass flowers:

standard carnation   *pixie carnation*

the arrangement to the focal area. The height of each bloom is varied to create a linear effect and to develop rhythm within the design. Some examples of mass flowers are roses, chrysanthemums, carnations, asters, tulips, daisies, dahlias, and peonies (also see page 56).

tulip

AND

gerbera   *marguerite daisy*

standard incurve chrysanthemum   *daisy chrysanthemum*

spray decorative chrysanthemum   *cushion pompon chrysanthemum*

Four well-known types of the foliage often used with massed flowers
are shown on the next page. Others that the flower arranger may select are
pittisporum, camellia leaves, caladium, ficus, dieffenbachia, and magnolia.

FIGURE 3–7 (continued)

Mass foliage:

lemon leaf (salal)

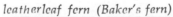

jade palm (wide leaf)

leatherleaf fern (Baker's fern)

emerald palm (narrow leaf)

Filler Flowers and Foliages: Filler flowers add a finishing touch to an arrangement (see Figure 3–8). Two types of filler flowers are used in flower arrangements: *bunch* and *feather*. Bunch-type filler flowers have many stems with small, mass-type heads. Examples of these are pompon chrysanthemums, button mums, asters, and sweet peas. Huckleberry foliage is used with this type of filler flower to aid in concealing holes and spaces in a design. Feather-type filler flowers add a misty or delicate appearance to a design. These create an arrangement that is softened by their light and airy forms. Some examples of feather-type filler flowers and foliage are statice, heather, babies' breath (*Gypsophila*), and the asparagus fern (*Asparagus plumosus*).

FIGURE 3–8   *Some representative Filler flowers and foliage types are shown on these pages and at the top of page 60.*

(a) Gypsophila (babies' breath)

(b) statice

(c) Asparagus sprengerii

(d) heather   (e) huckleberry

FIGURE 3–8 (continued)

(f) asparagus fern (Asparagus plumosus)

CARE AND CONDITIONING OF CUT FLOWERS

The keeping quality or flower longevity of cut flowers is of utmost importance to the florist and floral designer. The maintenance of cut-flower quality depends upon proper handling and care at each stage of the marketing channel. These include: (1) the proper culture of the plants by the grower, (2) harvesting at the correct stage of flower development, (3) speedy transportation from the grower to the wholesale florist, (4) proper handling and care of the flowers by the wholesale florist, (5) proper care and conditioning of the flowers by the retail florist, and (6) proper customer instruction in flower care. The retail florist must adequately care for cut-flower shipments if the flower quality is to be maintained.

Cut flowers are received regularly at flower shops from wholesale florists and greenhouses. Most cut flowers are shipped in special packing boxes to provide protection from weather and handling (see Figure 3–9). These flowers are shipped without water and may remain dry for some time, so it is essential that they are properly cared for immediately upon their arrival if the flowers are to remain fresh and healthy for arranging.

As the flowers are unpacked from the shipping container, the bunches are sorted onto tables, where they are unwrapped or untied and then placed in containers of water. These containers should be immediately placed in

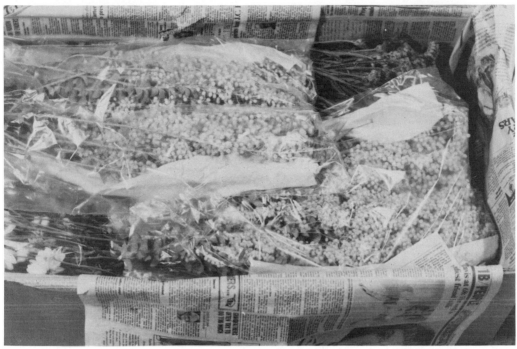

FIGURE 3–9   *A cut-flower shipment. Prompt unpacking, inspection, and refrigeration of fresh cut flowers are important in the preservation of the life of flowers.*

a refrigerated cooler while the remaining flowers are being unpacked. Once the entire shipment of flowers is unpacked and inspected for damage, individual containers of flowers are removed from refrigeration for further preparation.

Gladiolus are shipped in special cartons called *hampers* that allow the flowers to remain upright while in transit. These flowers are shipped in a tight-bud condition and must be held at room temperature for a short period to allow the blooms to open. The bunches of gladiolus are untied and the stems cut at the base. The gladiolus are then placed in large containers in 4 to 6 inches of preservative-water and held at room temperature for a few hours to allow the blooms to open slightly. They may then be placed in the storage refrigerator until needed.

The proper care and conditioning of cut flowers begins with using clean refrigerator containers. The holding water used for previously stored flowers should be discarded. The containers should then be cleaned with a solution of detergent, household bleach, and water to remove any bacterial scum and decayed plant litter. The containers are then refilled with tepid water (100–110° F, 38–43° C) since warm water contains less entrapped air than cold water. The air bubbles from the water can be taken into the vessels of the flower stems and cause a blockage to the uptake of water into the plant.

A flower preservative is added to the water in each storage container to aid in prolonging the life of the cut flowers (see Figure 3–10). Most commercial flower preservative compounds contain ingredients that reduce the growth of bacteria and provide a food source for the flowers. Sugar is included in these commercial preservatives to provide a source of carbohydrates to the flowers to extend their vase life. Bacterial growth must be controlled in holding solutions for cut flowers. The bacteria will foul the water where stems and leaves are in contact with the water and also may cause the plugging of the water-conducting tissues of the flower stem. This will cause the eventual wilting of the flowers. Although many home recipes have been suggested for preserving cut-flower quality, more satisfactory results are obtained from the use of commercially prepared floral preservatives containing 8-hydroxyquinoline citrate (8-HQC) and sugar. Flower containers manufactured from plastic, glass, or pottery should be used with such floral preservatives. Metal storage containers will rust and may inhibit the action of the preservative chemicals causing reduced life of the cut flowers.

FIGURE 3–10
Adding flower preservative. These compounds reduce the growth of bacteria and provide a food source for the cut flowers.

Before the cut flowers are ready for arranging, they must be properly conditioned to provide adequate water uptake into the stems and to keep the flowers healthy. The following procedures should be followed when preparing the flowers for proper conditioning:

Recut the Stems

Step 1: All cut-flower stems should receive a fresh cut before being placed in storage containers. This is done to ensure that water movement is not impeded by blocked stem vessels. For most herbaceous stems, a fresh cut may be made about 1–2 inches above the previously cut surface. A slanting cut made with a sharp, clean knife is recommended. This treatment will provide a greater surface area for water absorption and will allow water uptake when the stems reach to the bottom of the container. Many florists do not give each stem an individual slanted cut, because this requires additional time and effort. They may either trim the bottoms of the stems with a scissors or bunches of stems will be sliced by a knife on a chopping block. These stems should be recut every two days until the flowers are used in an arrangement or are sold.

Although the flower stems may be cut most rapidly using a shears or a knife on a chopping block, the best results are obtained when the stems are cut under water. Removing the lower portion of the stems in a large bucket of preservative-water will cause the stems to draw the solution into the water-conducting vessels. When this practice is not followed, the stem vessels will draw large air bubbles that will impede the uptake of water.

A common practice in the floral trade has been to crush the lower 1–2 inches of woody stems in order to enhance water uptake. This practice actually has no beneficial effect since woody stems are poor water conductors. These stems should either be recut more frequently or the woody portion of the stem removed to expose the succulent tissue to the water.

Seal Stems Having Milky Sap

Certain flower stems contain a sticky, milky sap that can reseal the cut surface as soon as it is dry. Such flowers as poinsettias are prepared for conditioning by first recutting the stem and then sealing the latex or milky sap. This may be done by either placing the freshly cut stem base in boiling water for a few seconds or by passing a flame under the cut stem surface to sear the sap. This procedure will cause the latex to congeal and allow better water uptake into the stem.

Bind Fleshy Stems

Certain types of fleshy stems become soft and split easily when placed in water containers. These stems should be wrapped with florist thread or string just above the cut surface to prevent damage to the stem. Flower stems that may require this treatment include irises, daffodils, tulips, and calla lilies.

Remove Excess Leaves and Thorns

Step 2: All foliage that will be below the water level in holding containers should be stripped from the stems. This practice will prevent the foliage from decaying and fouling the water. Rose thorns are removed as far up the stem as practical by cutting with a knife or a rose stem stripping tool. Removing the thorns makes the roses more easily handled and also prevents bruising of foliage and flower petals by puncturing from adjacent thorns during storage.

Use a Floral Preservative in Water

Step 3: A floral preservative is added to the holding water to help extend the cut-flower life. This floral preservative compound is measured into tepid water and stirred to dissolve it. Warm water is used for conditioning all cut flowers, which should then be placed in a refrigerator to prevent excessively rapid opening of the blooms.

The depth of the water in containers is generally between one-fourth and one-third the depth of the container. The height of the container used should not be any greater than the length of the flower stems below the blooms. Gladiolus stems are placed in only 4–6 inches of water in the holding containers because the foliage remains on these stems during storage.

Use Correct Refrigeration Conditions

Temperature: Not all cut flowers and foliage have the same temperature requirements during storage; but since only one refrigeration unit is generally all that is available, a compromise in temperature is used. The temperature that benefits the majority of the flowers held by a florist is 40° F (4.5° C), according to the U.S. Department of Agriculture. Orchids store best at 50° F (10° C), so they are kept separated from other flowers in a warmer location of the refrigerator. These flowers are stored in their original shipping boxes in water-filled tubes (orchid picks). It is strongly recommended that two refrigerators be used, however, with one set at 50° F and the other at 38° F.

Humidity, Air Circulation, and Light: The water evaporation from floral containers generally adds adequate humidity to the air to keep flowers in a fully turgid condition during refrigeration. If excessive molding or flower petal rotting is noticed, however, the floral containers require separation to allow better air circulation around the flowers. Vases should be loosely packed with the same types of flowers and separated from each other slightly to avoid most storage-related diseases from occurring. Nearly all cut flowers will benefit from the addition of artificial light during storage refrigeration. Since the cut flowers and foliages are still alive and maturing, using artificial fluorescent lighting is recommended during storage.

Sanitation: All old flowers, broken foliage, and litter should be removed from the storage refrigerator as soon as they are discovered. Foliage that has dropped onto the floor can cause the floor to become dangerously slick and will contribute to the aging of other flowers in the cooler. Flowers that have passed maturity also cause younger flowers to mature more rapidly from the emission of ethylene gas, a natural product of the aging process of flowers. All old, damaged, or diseased flowers should be removed from the storage containers to decrease the ethylene content of the air inside the refrigerator.

Certain flower types produce more ethylene gas than others. It is advantageous to provide a separate storage cooler for these flowers, if possible, to prevent excessive ethylene in the air around more sensitive flowers. Orchids, carnations, snapdragons, and calla lilies are heavy producers of ethylene in storage refrigerators. Most cut-foliage should also be stored separately. Fruits and vegetables produce very high amounts of ethylene gas in storage and should *never* be kept with cut flowers. Modern floral coolers are equipped with ethylene scrubbers or filters to remove this harmful gas.

Storage of Cut Foliage

In Water Containers: The following cut-foliage may be placed in lukewarm water and refrigerated in the same manner as cut flowers: eucalyptus, jade leaf, emerald leaf, and podocarpus. Using plastic wrap is recommended for both croton and ti leaves in water containers.

In Packing Cartons: The following cut foliage types are lightly sprinkled with water and left in the original plastic-lined packing box in the refrigerator: leatherleaf (Baker's fern), asparagus fern, huckleberry, salal, and ivy.

CARE OF CUT FLOWERS FROM THE GARDEN

The floral designer should be aware of the correct methods for preparing flowers that are obtained from the field, greenhouse, or garden. Many florists grow some of their own flowers for use in the flower shop, especially during the warmer seasons. Floral designers may also be consulted on the proper methods for caring for cut flowers that are grown in the customers' gardens. These flowers will also require the proper conditioning treatment if long-lasting flower arrangements are to be obtained. The key to proper conditioning of cut flowers grown in the garden or greenhouse is to cut them at the correct stage of flower bud development.

Stage of Development for Cutting Flowers

Fully Developed Flowers: Most composite flower types will not become any larger or more developed after cutting. Examples are chrysanthemums, daisies, asters, and dahlias.

Half-open Blooms: Spike flower types will continue to develop and add life to an arrangement when cut with only about one-half of the florets open. Examples are gladiolus, snapdragons, larkspur, and delphinium.

Bud Stage: The single type flowers will often continue to develop after cutting. Examples are irises, jonquils, tulips, roses, peonies, and poppies.

Cut-flower Stem Length

The plant's growth habit determines the length of stem to be cut. Plants grown as a single stem or to produce only a single flower are usually cut at the maximum length. Some examples of these are snapdragons, chrysanthemums, tulips, irises, gladiolus, lilies, and jonquils.

Plants that normally produce more than one flower at a time on a plant will generally bloom over extended periods. When cutting stems on these plants, consideration must be given to the general vigor of the plant and to future blooming potential. The stems of such flowers as roses and carnations are cut at a level that will provide an adequate stem length for arranging without reducing the blooming ability of the plant.

Flowers that are cut in the early morning or during evening hours generally will be fully turgid and will contain adequate carbohydrate food reserves. Cutting flowers during the hottest portion of the day should be avoided, since the stems and foliage will often wilt easily. For greatest use in floral arrangements, most flowers should be cut while in the young bud stage, just as the petals are showing color.

After the flowers are cut, the stems should be prepared in the same manner as described earlier for those at a flower shop. Tepid water and a commercial floral preservative are combined and added to tall floral vases. The newly cut flowers are placed in the vases with the stems submerged to a level that covers one-third to one-half the stems. The vases of flowers are then placed in a cool, dark area that is free from drafts overnight to allow the stems to absorb the maximum amount of water. Flowers that have received this treatment will be properly conditioned for arranging the following morning.

The flowers in an arrangement will last much longer if they are provided with special care in the home. The water in the arrangement's container should be refilled each day using a floral preservative. If any of the flowers become limp and flaccid, they should be removed from the arrangement, given a fresh cut on the stem, and then completely submerged in water for several hours. This treatment will generally restore the flower and stem to its fully turgid condition and it may be replaced in the arrangement. Flower arrangements should be placed in a cool, dark location during the night to help the blooms conserve water. They would benefit from being placed outdoors, when practical, to be exposed to the cool, damp air. When moving the arrangements to another location is not practical, the water content of the flowers may be maintained by placing a polyethylene bag over the design during the evening hours or placing them in a food refrigerator. Periodic misting of the flowers in the arrangement is also somewhat beneficial in maintaining the turgidity of the blooms.

SELECTING FLORAL CONTAINERS

Selecting the proper container to be used for a specific flower arrangement is very important when creating a suitable design (see Figure 3–11). The container becomes an integral part of the floral composition and is the starting point or foundation of a design. Since the character of the container can greatly influence the mood of the arrangement, it must be chosen carefully. A properly selected container will be functional, will suggest the mood of the design, will not detract from the flowers, and will help create harmony and unity in the arrangement.

Function

The container selected should be suitable for arranging flowers. It must be capable of holding water, be stable enough to support the weight of the flowers, and be deep enough to hold an adequate supply of water. The opening at the top of an upright container should be large enough to accommodate the required number and sizes of stems to be used. Low, flat containers should have a suitable depth to hold adequate amounts of water for the flowers in the arrangement. These low containers are suitable for home designs, but are not usually used by florists because the water is spilled easily during delivery of the arrangements.

The customary materials used in floral design container construction are glass, metal, plastic, porcelain, or glazed pottery. Glass containers are more satisfactory if they are translucent, since clear glass shows the masses of cut stems from the flowers below the water. These stems are difficult to disguise and detract from the floral arrangement. Metallic finishes require protection from the tarnishing that accompanies the use of floral preservative chemicals in the container water. A plastic sheet may be used as a liner to protect the finish before a floral foam or stems are placed in the container. When pottery containers are to be used, the glaze should extend across the bottom surface on the outside of the piece. This glazed surface is preferred to prevent a "sweating" or moisture accumulation that may damage wood surfaces when water is placed in the container.

Commercial florists use many container styles constructed from papier-mâché for their more utilitarian designs. These containers will provide a suitable method for holding water for most floral designs. The inside bottom surface of the container is coated with asphalt to provide extra protection from water leakage. Since this container is constructed from paper, it should be discarded after its initial use.

Style

The shape and size of a container often suggests the type of design to be created within it. A large, heavy container requires a taller arrangement to balance the mass of the container. A beautiful curved style of arrangement calls for a dainty stemmed compote to provide balance. A horizontal dinner table arrangement is most attractive when constructed in a low, flat rectangular container. The lines of the container are repeated or accentuated to provide unity and harmony within the design.

Harmony is created within a design composition when the container becomes an integral part of the arrangement. In order to achieve harmony, a container must be of the proper size and scale to create a balanced relationship. Generally, the rules of floral design dictate that for an upright arrangement, the tallest flower should be approximately one and one-half times the height of the container. In low or horizontal designs in flat containers, the length of the design is the sum of the length and width of the container. These height and width relationships are used as a guide only and need not be followed for all designs.

A container is selected for its compatibility with the intended use of the arrangement. For example, a formal design might call for an elegant container used with dainty flowers. The texture of the container must be repeated in the flower types used in the arrangement. A coarse-textured wood or pottery container appears best when this coarseness is repeated in the flowers. Similarly, fine-textured flowers appear best when a container having simple lines or textures is selected.

Color

The color of a container should be compatible with those found in the flowers used to create a floral arrangement. The color pattern found in the container appears best when it either repeats those found in the color scheme of the design or when neutral colors are present in the container. The most utilitarian colors used in floral containers are green, white, gray, brown, tan, or black. These container colors are compatible with most any floral design color scheme when used properly. Green-colored floral vases are often selected, since nearly all flower stems and foliage repeat this color. Brown containers appear best when this color is duplicated in dried flowers, wood, or autumn-colored leaves. Brightly colored and ornate floral containers have a limited use in floral design, since they attract attention and are difficult to harmonize in color schemes. Both black and white colored containers should be used with caution. These colors will draw attention to the base of the arrangement and away from the focal area unless properly balanced by the flower colors in the design.

Metallic containers having a finish of silver, brass, bronze, and gold leaf usually suggest a formal design. The flower colors used with these containers is very important if harmony and unity of the design are to be preserved. The yellow and yellow-red tones of the gold, brass, and bronze should be repeated in the flowers to blend the container to the design. Flowers having blue, lavender, or white colors create a pleasing mood when used with a silver container. When colors are used improperly between the container and flowers, each element becomes separated and unity of the design is lost.

STEM SUPPORTS

The various types of containers used for flower arrangements require some method for securely anchoring the flower stems. In selecting an adequate holder, the arranger should consider the style of the container, the plant material to be used, and the finished arrangement style. A properly selected stem support will provide the freedom of stem placement in any desired position and will hold them securely for the useful life of the arrangement. Many styles and types of flower stem supporting devices are used by florists or sold by department stores. Some stem supports and their uses are described.

Needlepoint Holders: Needlepoint holders are also called *pin* holders or *frogs.* They are rarely used in commercial florists' designing, but are popular stem-supporting aids for home flower arranging. Needlepoint holders are customarily used for the creation of modernistic and stylized

FIGURE 3–12   *Examples of*
needlepoint holders.

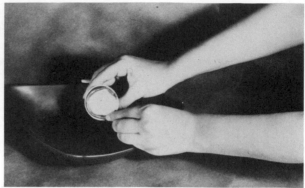

FIGURE 3–13   *A clay rope around the*
base anchors the holder.

designs by the home arranger. These pin holders offer a versatility of design where fewer flowers are to be used, since less of the holder must be
concealed by foliage. Florists prefer not to use needlepoint holders because
flower stems are not anchored as securely as with other support materials
and water is easily spilled from the arrangements during delivery.

A needlepoint holder consists of many inverted, closely spaced,
sharp-pointed nails that are anchored to a heavy base (see Figure 3–12).
The flower stems may be stuck directly onto the pins or they may be
wedged between them. When small stems are to be inserted between the
points, a larger stem may be wedged against them for anchorage. Also,
several smaller stems may be bound together with string or a rubber band
to provide the necessary surface area to secure them to the pin holder.
Large woody stems may be anchored more securely if the stem base is split
before it is inserted on the needlepoint holder. When stems are placed on
a needlepoint holder, the stem bases should always be below the water
level in the container.

Needlepoint holders are available in many sizes and shapes (round,
oval, or square) to suit any particular arranging requirements. They may
be placed in any location at the base of the container and anchored for
temporary or permanent use. The holder is secured to a container with
either floral clay or a tight-sealing floral adhesive. The bottom of the container must be cleaned and thoroughly dried before the clay and holder
will tightly adhere to it. A thin rope of clay is formed by rolling it between
the palms of both hands. Place the clay rope around the outside perimeter
of the needlepoint base and press it firmly to the container in the desired
position (see Figure 3–13). The seal is tested by carefully lifting the container by the holder. If the pinholder pulls free easily from the container,
the surface must be cleaned again to remove any remaining oil or dirt.

FIGURE 3–14   *Large flower stem supports. Chicken wire with a filler material is sometimes used for large arrangements in papier-maché containers.*

Chicken Wire: Large arrangements or bouquets having heavy flowers require a firm support for the tall stems that are placed in deep containers. The stems should be submerged to a depth of 4–6 inches and must not slip out of place during delivery or handling. The stem support aid used for these large floral bouquets usually consists of *chicken wire* and a *filler* material (see Figure 3–14). The chicken wire or floral netting of enameled green wire having a 1-inch mesh is generally used. The filler material may be of shredded styrofoam plastic, chipped floral foam, vermiculite, or the wire may be used to cover a solid block of floral foam.

The shredded filler material is first pressed firmly into the cavity of the container. A layer of chicken wire is then placed over the top of the filler material. The wire is prepared by cutting a square with wire cutters and then molding it to form a loose ball that will fit the opening of the container. The ball of wire should be crushed and rolled until it forms a mass of layers that will allow each stem to pass through at least three meshes of wire for firm support. The wire is then wedged securely to the sides of the container with 2–3 inches of wire exposed above the container rim. The floral netting will prevent the filler material from floating out of the container when water is added. It will also serve as a strong anchor for the large stems that are to be inserted into the arrangement.

FIGURE 3–15   *A selection of floral foams for cut flower arrangements.*

Floral Foams: The various floral foam products are currently very popular stem-supporting aids for both florist and home flower arrangements. These floral foams are manufactured from resins in several shapes, colors, and for various design purposes (see Figure 3–15). For example, a soft-textured foam is used for soft and smaller-stemmed flowers. Other grades are used with standard and heavy-stemmed flowers. Floral foams are also sold in a wide array of colors for more decorative and creative designs. They may be purchased in either rectangular bricks to be cut to fit individual containers, or they are also available in cylindrical blocks for use in specialized containers. Many of the floral foam products do not contain a floral preservative and sugar to aid in extending cut-flower life. These products are extremely porous, so they provide water to the inserted flower stems used in the arrangement.

The foam blocks must be thoroughly saturated with water before being used to support fresh flowers. The quick-filling floral foams may be simply placed in a bucket filled with preservative and water. After a few minutes, the top of the foam block will sink to the water surface. These floral foam blocks should not be used until they are completely saturated with water, or severe flower wilting will occur.

When containers that are specially designed for anchoring floral foam blocks are used, the foam is simply pressed into the holder provided at the base of the container. When these foams are used with other styles of containers, other anchoring methods may be required. The foam blocks are cut to fit small-mouthed containers and then pressed into the opening. A small wedge-shaped opening is cut from the block to provide a space for adding water to the container. The foam block is inserted to a depth that leaves 1–2 inches of the block extended above the lip of the container for easier arranging and to provide a more attractive design.

FIGURE 3–16   *Floral foam is anchored with a water-resistant adhesive tape in some containers.*

When large containers are used for arranging, the foam may not be anchored securely by merely pressing it into the cavity. A water-resistant floral adhesive tape is required for holding the foam block in place. The lip of the container must be thoroughly cleaned and dried before the tape is applied. A single strip of tape is placed over the foam block and secured over the lip of the container (see Figure 3–16). In cases where large foam blocks are required, more than one strip of tape may be necessary. The tape that extends over the lip of the container may be easily concealed with foliage or ribbon when the flowers are arranged.

Under certain conditions, it may not be practical to use floral adhesive tape to secure the foam to the container. Floral foam blocks may be held in glass or porcelain containers by plastic holders that are adhered to the container base by use of floral clay or other adhesives (see Figure 3–17). These plastic holders firmly secure floral foams in such containers as low, flat dishes, where the use of adhesive tape would be unattractive. In other instances, where large-stemmed flowers and large blocks of foam are required, the floral foam may be adequately held in place by using a square of chicken wire (floral netting). The wire is cut to a size that is slightly larger than the container top and folded until the wire is firmly secured.

The container and floral foam should be kept filled with water while the arrangement is being constructed. The flower stems should be inserted

FIGURE 3–17   *Floral foam blocks may be supported by use of a plastic holder that is anchored to the container with floral clay.*

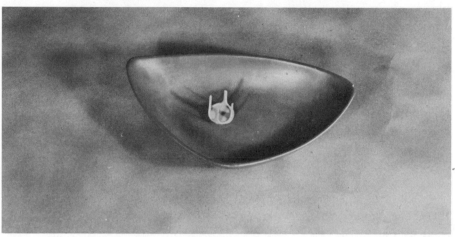

as deeply into the foam as practical and should extend into the water for best results. Flower stems should be cut to a slanted base before inserting them into the foam. This slanted cut will expose more of the base to the foam and water and will aid in providing a firm anchorage. Once the stem is inserted in the floral foam, it should not be pulled backward in the hole. Doing this will remove the stem base from contact with the foam and perhaps from the water. Use of these floral foam products requires a certain amount of practice in flower arranging. Once a stem is placed in the foam, it should not be removed and reinserted. Excessive rearranging of stems in the floral design can cause the foam product to disintegrate to a point where it will no longer anchor the stems securely.

WIRING CUT-FLOWER STEMS

Flower stems sometimes require wire to add support in an arrangement. Although most flowers will not require this treatment, flower stems are wired by the florist for several important reasons. Adding a stiff wire to a stem may prevent a blossom from being inadvertently broken during delivery or handling. As flowers age, they become weak in the stems. Adding a support wire will hold the bloom erect after the stem can no longer provide adequate strength. Wire is also used to combine several blooms together to create a massed effect. One of the most important reasons for wiring flowers is for the purpose of straightening a crooked stem or to add a curve to an otherwise straight stem. Using wire allows the designer to create the desired curves and lines in an arrangement.

Florist wire is available either in enameled green or as unpainted wire strands. The green enameled wire is preferred since it will not rust and blends nicely with most flower stems. The wire is sold in 6-, 12-, and 18-inch lengths in boxes containing up to 12 pounds of wire. The wire thicknesses used for floral arranging range from the larger diameter of no. 16 gauge to the very thin wire of no. 36 gauge. Most florists will use two gauges of heavy wire (no. 16 to no. 22) and several thicknesses of light wire (no. 24 to no. 36). The heavier wire gauges are used primarily for reinforcing large stems in arrangements. The lighter gauges of wire are used most often in constructing corsages and in wedding designs.

Wire Sizes for Flower Stem Support

The size of wire is listed according to its gauge number. The higher the gauge number, the finer the wire. The most frequently used sizes and their uses are:

Wire Size (No.)	*Most Frequent Uses*
16 and 18	Heavy wire used to support large flower stems or heavy flowers such as lilies, snapdragons, or gladiolus.
20 and 22	Mediumweight wire used to support such flowers as roses, carnations, and chrysanthemums.
24 and 26	Lightweight wire used for replacing flower stems in corsages and wedding bouquets.
28 and 30	Very fine wire used for delicate corsage work and for reinforcing stems already supported with a heavier wire.
32 and 36	Ultrafine wire used in constructing glamellias, dainty corsages, and wedding bouquets.

Wiring Methods for Flower Arrangements

Fresh flower stems are wired by several methods, depending on the flower type and the preferences of the designer. The most common wiring techniques include the straight wire, hook wire, and insertion methods.

Straight Wire Method: Roses, carnations, and other similar mass-type flowers having solid stems are supported by inserting the wire into the base of the calyx with remaining wire loosely wound around the flower stem (see Figure 3–18). The wire is wound carefully between the leaves in a manner that will leave the wire as straight as possible. The remaining

FIGURE 3–18 *Wiring flower stems for arrangements. (a) Loosely wrapped wire is used for roses and carnations. (b) Insert a wire through the center of fleshy-stemmed flowers. (c) The hook method is used for flat-headed flowers such as daisies and chrysanthemums.*

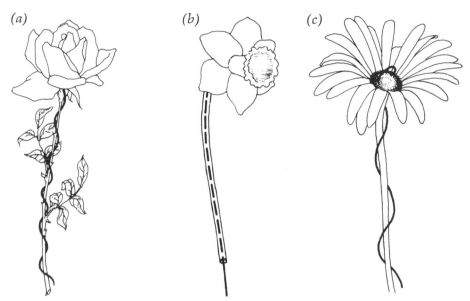

(a) *(b)* *(c)*

wire at the base of the stem is carefully clipped and the flower stem inserted into the stem holder by holding the wire against the stem. If this is done properly, the wire will not gouge a hole in the floral foam, if this material is used. This procedure is better than allowing the trailing wire to extend back up the stem. Whenever flowers are wired for use in arrangements, the wires are to be concealed by foliage or flowers.

Hook Wire Method: Flowers with flattened heads on weak stems (such as pompon chrysanthemums and daisies) may be supported by first running the end of the wire completely through the flower at a point near the stem attachment to the calyx. A small hook is shaped at the end of the wire which is then pulled back into the center of the petals until it is secured and hidden from view. The designer must be careful that the wire is not pulled with a force great enough to break the flower. The wire is then run down the length of the stem and secured at the base.

Insertion Method: Larger, fleshy-stemmed, or hollow-stemmed flowers (such as tulips, jonquils, irises, and gladiolus) are supported by inserting the wire through the center of the stem to the base of the flower head. The wire is pushed against the calyx until it is firmly set, but without forcing the end of the wire through the flower. The excess wire below the stem base is clipped before the stem is placed in the container.

SELECTED REFERENCES

BENZ, M. *Flowers: Geometric Form*, 3rd ed. Houston, Tex.: San Jacinto Publishing Company, 1966.

CUTLER, K. N. *How to Arrange Flowers for all Occasions*. Garden City, N.Y.: Doubleday & Company, Inc., 1967.

FORT, V. P. *A Complete Guide to Flower Arrangement*. New York: Viking Press, 1962.

GOLDEN, W. P., ed. *Cut Flower Care Guide*. Florist, Vol. 12, No. 10, pp. 41–89.

GORDON, R. L. *Professional Flower Arranging for Beginners*. New York: Arco Publishing Company, 1974.

HILLIER, F. B. *Basic Guide to Flower Arranging*. New York: McGraw-Hill Book Company, 1974.

McDANIEL, G. L. *Ornamental Horticulture*. Reston, Va.: Reston Publishing Company, 1979.

PFAHL, P. B. *The Retail Florist Business*. Danville, Ill.: Interstate Printers and Publishers, Inc., 1968.

STRATMAN, T. S. *Retail Floriculture, Book II: Designing and Care of Flowers and Foliage*. Ohio Agricultural Education Curriculum Materials Service. Columbus: Ohio State University, 1976.

TERMS TO KNOW

Compote	Floret	Line flowers
Filler flowers	Flower conditioning	Mass flowers
Floral foam	Form flowers	Needlepoint holder
Floral preservative	Latex	Spike flowers

STUDY QUESTIONS

1. Describe the various methods of conditioning cut flowers before they are used in a flower arrangement.
2. List the desirable characteristics of a flower container. Explain how the size, shape, color, and texture of a container can influence the design of a flower arrangement.
3. Discuss the use of various flower types in a flower arrangement according to the flower classifications: line, form, mass, and filler.
4. Explain why it is necessary to add support wires to some flower stems in an arrangement, while it is not required for others.

SUGGESTED ACTIVITIES

1. Compare the useful lives of cut flowers that have been properly conditioned with others that have not. In your comparisons, set up floral containers having tap water and others containing the proper amount of a commercially prepared flower preservative. Place flowers in the containers with both properly prepared stem ends and others that have not been given a treatment to allow adequate water uptake. Record the number of days each flower survives in healthy condition for each flower species and treatment method.
2. Practice wiring various flower types using the three methods described in this chapter.
3. Set up a display of flower arranging containers that shows both good and poor styles. Discuss the various features of these containers in class as they pertain to design and function in flower arranging.
4. Make a poster as a class project that shows each of the most common florist flower and foliage types used in flower arrangements. Group these plant materials according to their classifications. For this exercise, pictures may be cut from magazines or black and white pictures may be used and then mounted on the poster board.

UNIT II:

Floral Design Methods

82

CHAPTER 4:

Basic Floral Arrangements

The beginning floral designer must become familiar with the basic techniques involved in handling fresh flowers and foliages in the construction of flower arrangements. This chapter describes the various basic arrangement styles used in contemporary floral design. The student designer should master each design style in the order that they are presented. By doing this, the skills required for mastering each design style will be accumulated until more individual freedom of expression in designing with flowers is attained. Students should follow the outlined construction procedures for each design style, using both the verbal and pictorial descriptions.

The Designer's Assistant

In a retail flower shop, the beginning designer's assistant will most likely be responsible for preparing the containers and cut flowers to be used by the designer in arrangements. As assistant designers gain the skills and knowledge necessary for design work, they may be given the responsibility for arranging some basic pieces. The techniques required for constructing these arrangements are easily learned. However, before more complicated arrangements may be attempted, student designers must be able to create pleasing designs both rapidly and accurately. This period of training is challenging and rewarding for the ambitious and creative student designer.

BASIC FLORAL DESIGN STYLES

Flower arrangements are more pleasing to the eye when their outline creates a geometric pattern. The basic shape of the arrangement establishes the line and creates unity of the design, whether it is traditional or modern-abstract in style. The silhouette of the arrangement is the framework from which the floral composition is constructed. The proper establishment of the floral framework makes the difference between a planned floral design and flowers that are merely placed in a container.

The beginning floral designer should visualize the completed floral design before starting the arrangement by comparing it to a geometrical shape. The basic outline of the arrangement is then determined, keeping this geometrical pattern in mind. The *skeleton* flowers are those that set the geometrical limits or boundaries for a design. For one-sided arrangements, three skeleton flowers are used to determine the height and width of the design style. These flower stems may vary in length, but will aid the arranger in the creation of balance and proportion within the design.

The most common geometric shapes used in florist's designs include those shown on these two pages in Figure 4–1.

FIGURE 4–1
Shapes in floral designs.

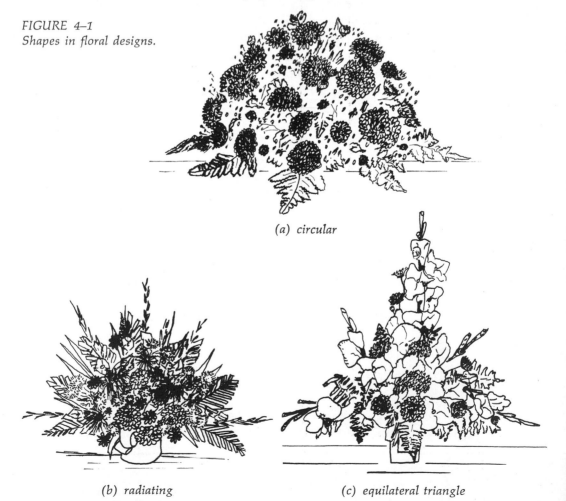

(a) circular

(b) radiating

(c) equilateral triangle

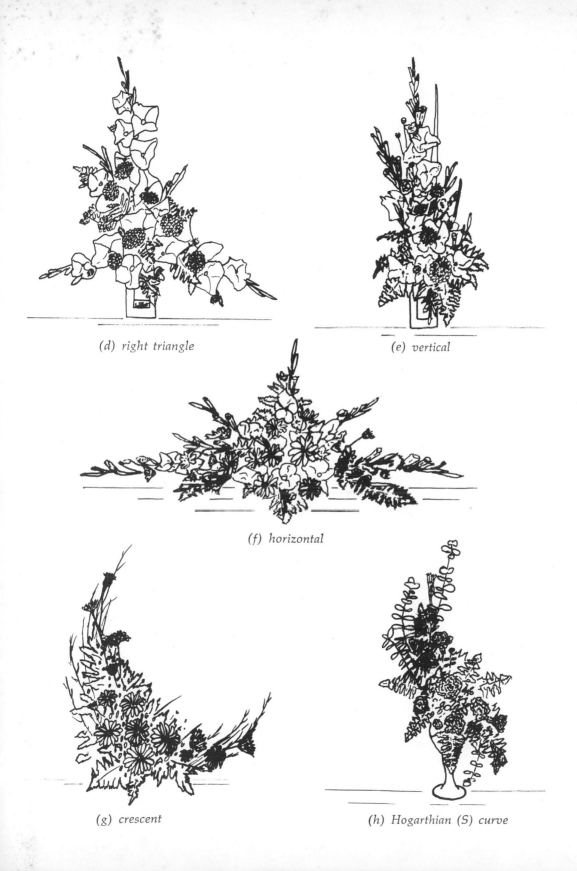

(d) right triangle

(e) vertical

(f) horizontal

(g) crescent

(h) Hogarthian (S) curve

Circular Designs

The circular design is arranged to form a round centerpiece that appears the same on all sides. This design is easiest for the beginning flower arranger because it does not require the placement of a focal point. The circular style of design allows the novice designer an opportunity to handle fresh flowers and to become accustomed to the basic principles of flower arranging.

Circular designs are widely used in decorating because they are relatively simple to construct and serve many decoration purposes. The circular design will make an excellent centerpiece for a low table and for dinner or reception parties. These arrangements may be constructed so as to be viewed from only one side. However, they are usually designed to be seen from all sides (*all-around* designs). When designed to be viewed from any side, these arrangements are especially attractive when placed in front of a mirror.

Circular designs are normally constructed in low, round containers, or they may be arranged in baskets fitted with inserts that hold water. The shape of the design is determined by making each of the skeleton flowers of equal length and placing these in position at the top, front, back, and both sides of the arrangement. Each successive flower is then positioned so that the stem lengths will be the same as the skeleton flowers. The foliage is placed between the flowers to give a natural appearance and to cover the flower stems and holder. The circular design will not have a focal point when it is arranged to be viewed from all sides. Since the design appears best from the top, the same sizes of flowers may be used in the construction of a circular centerpiece arrangement.

Constructing a Circular Design: The procedures used in constructing a basic circular design are outlined in this section. The flowers selected for this design may be either *form* or *mass* flowers, along with some appropriate *filler* flowers, if desired. Spike-type flowers are not suitable for this style of design. Some typical flowers that are appropriate for the circular design include roses, chrysanthemums, daisies, tulips, irises, poppies, miniature carnations (pixies), and other similar flower types. The basic steps in constructing the all around circular design are explained next. See also the four photographs in Figure 4–1.

Step 1: Select a suitable round container that will provide the correct size relationship with the desired finished arrangement. A container that may be used with a floral foam product is most desirable for this design.

Step 2: Cut a block of floral foam to a size that will allow it to fit snugly in the container opening and will allow water to be added to the container reservoir. The top of the floral foam block should extend above the rim of the container to a height that will allow the flower stems to be placed in a horizontal position in the arrangement. Completely saturate the floral foam block, place it firmly in the container, and add water to the container reservoir.

Step 3: Place the foliage in the container before the flowers are added. This is done to create the basic shape of the arrangement, to conceal the floral foam or stem anchor, and to provide a more natural appearance for the flowers. Establish the height and width of the arrangement by the size of foliage stems to be used. Leather leaf fern is the most satisfactory foliage for use in this design style. The foliage stems are placed at the top, each side, and the front and back of the design (5 stems required). The top stem will be slightly taller than the sides to create a mounded appearance. The horizontally placed foliage stems may be placed so they lean slightly downward at their tips to hide the rim of the container.

Step 4: Add the foliage between the initially inserted foliage stems until the block is covered. Break the fern stems into smaller pieces to allow filling in the basic shape of the design without crowding. When done properly, no other foliage will be required once the flowers are added to the arrangement. Normally, only about eight standard-sized stems of leather leaf fern fronds will be required for a typical circular design to be viewed from all sides.

Step 5: Once the foliage is in place in the design, add the flowers. Add five flowers in the same manner as the greenery: at the top, each side, and at the front and back. These should form a slightly mounded circular shape. When viewed from above, a square should be formed by the horizontally placed flowers. These flowers may lean slightly downward, away from the foam block.

Step 6: Add the remaining flowers to the design until the shape is completely filled. Space the flowers adequately to provide an informal appearance and to allow the foliage to extend through the flowers. It should not be necessary for the individual flowers to touch each other in this design. It is very important not to mass these flowers together in tight bunches or the graceful, natural appearance will be lost in the design.

Step 7: Place the flowers randomly throughout the design to fill the voids between the skeleton flowers. Obvious patterns, such as lines or circles, created by the placement of flowers should be avoided. When

FIGURE 4–2 Constructing a circular design.

(a) Create the basic circular shape with foliage.   *(b) Establish the circular form with the skeleton flowers.*

two or more colors are used together in this design, be particularly careful to avoid obvious lines or segregations of colors within this style of arrangement. When viewed from above and from the sides, each flower should conform to the circular pattern of the arrangement. No flattened sides or extended flower stems should be apparent when the flowers are all in place.

Step 8: If desired, add a filler flower type to complete the circular design. Baby's breath (Gypsophila), statice, heather, or button chrysanthemums are most often used for this purpose. Use Gypsophila sparingly to create a soft, airy finishing touch to the design. Separate individual stem pieces of Gypsophila and place them carefully between the flowers in the arrangement. Arrange the individual florets carefully to allow them to protrude around the flowers and foliage. Add these stems until they are evenly placed throughout the body of the design, without appearing crowded.

Step 9: When the circular design is completed to the satisfaction of the arranger, mist the flowers and foliage lightly. This arrangement style should be mastered before the more difficult design styles are attempted. Beginning floral designers will find this design style is very popular in flower shops and can be used in many situations where a quick and simply constructed arrangement is required.

(c) *Randomly place the remaining flowers*
within the established outline.

(d) *Complete the design by adding*
a suitable filler flower, if desired.

Triangular Designs

The triangular designs are more often thought of as the traditional florist's bouquet styles. These balanced designs may be found in two basic forms: symmetrical or *formal* and asymmetrical or *informal.* The symmetrical design nearly creates a mirror image between the left and right sides of the arrangement. The asymmetrical design creates a more informal balance, with the visual weight shifted to one side.

Triangular-shaped designs are best created by using a mixture of mass or form, line, and filler flowers. Although triangular-shaped designs can be created without using spike-type flowers, the beginning flower arranger will find these flower types are helpful in determining the shape of the arrangement. Gladiolus, snapdragons, stocks, delphinium, or linear-shaped flowering branches are most commonly used in these designs. The typical triangular design styles include those called *radiating, equilateral triangle, right triangle, horizontal,* and *vertical.*

Radiating Designs: The radiating design style forms a fan-shaped outline. This one-sided design is used extensively for the larger arrangements at large group affairs where a dramatic accent is required. This is a traditional design for use at weddings, funerals, commencements, and on church altars.

Line flowers and foliages are used to form the fan-shaped outline. Florists use gladiolus, snapdragons, flat fern, and palm fronds most often for this purpose. The height of the arrangement is established first. After the width of the design is determined by the placement of flowers at each side, the fan shape is created by placing additional line flowers or foliage across the back to provide a rounded appearance. The radiating design is constructed by the following method (see Figure 4–3):

Step 1: Select a container that will allow for deep penetration of heavy stems and will support the weight of the long-stemmed flowers. Florists often use ceramic or papier-mâché containers filled with shredded styrofoam and chicken wire to lend added support. The heavy-duty floral foams are satisfactory if they are to be used on smaller designs; otherwise, they should be reinforced with folded chicken wire wrapped around the block of foam. If it is practical, allow the foam to extend above the rim of the container to enable stems to be placed horizontally in the container.

Step 2: First establish the height and width of the design by placing the line flowers at the top and both sides of the arrangement. These first three spike flowers will create the skeleton of the design and will form a triangular outline. Place the centrally located flower as far to the rear of the container as possible for anchorage. This will allow ample space for the placement of other large-stemmed flowers in front of it in the container. Also, tip the stem of the center flower toward the back slightly to allow the arrangement to attain depth.

FIGURE 4–3   Constructing a radiating design.

*(a) Establish
the basic outline
with the skeleton flowers.*

(b) Create the fan shape by adding flowers between the skeleton flowers.

(c) Fill the center of the arrangement with filler flowers.

Step 3: Complete the fan-shaped background by placing additional line flowers across the back. Shorten these flowers slightly from the top to sides as they are placed in the container to keep the outline rounded. Place additional flowers of the same type in the center of the design and in front of the skeleton flowers to fill the arrangement.

Step 4: Next add the focal point or accent area. This often includes a large bow constructed from no. 40 or no. 120 ribbon in larger florists' bouquets. Then mix mass-type flowers (such as roses, chrysanthemums, or carnations) among the spike flowers in the center on the arrangement. Mass these somewhat around the bow to create a distinct accent area at the front of the arrangement. These accent flowers will extend in front of the lip of the container so that the entire design displays depth and fullness.

Step 5: Add the foliage at any time during construction of the design. Generally, it is added sparingly after placing the skeleton flowers in position. Some additional foliage may be required once the flowers have been placed in the design. A successful design is not complete until foliage has been placed in the back of the arrangement to conceal the masses of stems and the stem holder.

FIGURE 4–3 (continued)

(d) Add the accent flowers and a bow, if desired.

(e) Place the background foliage behind the flowers to complete the design.

The beginning floral arranger must be particularly careful to avoid creating a lack of unity with the radiating design. The flowers that are selected to form the fan-shaped background must be repeated throughout the entire design. A lack of unity will result, for example, when gladiolus are used to create the skeleton of the arrangement and carnations or chrysanthemums are used to fill out the center of the design.

Equilateral Triangular Design: The equilateral triangular arrangement will have three primary axis flowers that create a truly triangular outline in the design. These are constructed to be placed against a wall or a backdrop and to serve as a room accent. An equilateral triangle-shaped arrangement will be as tall as it is wide. The tallest flower is placed exactly in the center of the container and as far to the rear of the holder as possible. The two skeleton flowers are then placed at each side. These horizontally placed flower stems should have a total length equal to the height of the central, vertically placed flower. A short-stemmed line flower is placed at the front of the arrangement so that it extends downward slightly from the horizontal angle with the rim of the container. The focal flower is positioned immediately above this line flower. The triangular arrangement is completed by filling in with the remaining flowers and foliage. A typical equilateral triangular design is constructed in the following manner (see Figure 4–4):

Step 1: Select a suitable container for this design as described for the radiating design.

Step 2: Place the three skeleton flowers in the container at the top and sides of the design. The length of the combined horizontally placed flowers equals the length of the centrally placed flower at the top.

Step 3: Place the short-stemmed line flower at the front of the arrangement so that it extends downward away from the lip of the container.

Step 4: Add foliage to provide a background and to fill in the center of the design loosely. The foliage should not be packed, but rather loosely arranged to conceal the stems and stem holder. Properly placed foliage will extend up and around the flowers in a finished arrangement.

Step 5: Next, add the focal flowers in the area in front of and immediately above the rim of the container. These flowers should not be crowded together, but rather loosely arranged to show their individual character. If a bow is chosen to enhance the focal area, place it in the container before the focal flowers are added. Then place the flowers around and through the bow to reduce its contrast with the flowers in the arrangement.

Step 6: Complete the arrangement by adding the mass flowers and remaining line flowers to the center of the design. If desired, add foliage to conceal any remaining holes in the arrangement. Finally, finish the back of the design to add a professional touch to it.

FIGURE 4–4   *Constructing an equilateral-triangle design.*

(a) Establish the outline of the triangle with the first four flowers.

(b) Place the foliage and remaining spike flowers in the center of the design.

(c) Complete the design by inserting the focal flowers and filler material.

Right-Triangular Design: The right-triangular or asymmetrical floral design is constructed in a manner similar to the equilateral triangular design. However, one side of the arrangement will appear to be visually heavier than the other (see Figure 4–5). Because these designs indicate a direction, they can be used to emphasize lines in a room or window display. For example, paired right- and left-handed triangular designs may be placed on a fireplace mantle to accent a picture. The method used in the construction of a typical right triangle arrangement is outlined next:

Step 1: You may construct the right-triangle style of design in any number of container types. It is best constructed in a container having an oval or rectangular shape. The container may be either low and shallow or it may be an upright stemmed style. In either case, the container must be capable of supporting the heavy stems and accepting a suitable stem holder for the flowers.

Step 2: In the asymmetrical arrangement, the three skeleton flowers are of unequal length. Place the tallest flower to the left of the center and to the rear of the container. Determine the height of the tallest flower by the container and the type of flowers selected for the design, but it may be as much as twice the height of the container.

Step 3: The right-side, horizontally placed flower stem will be approximately two-thirds the length of the tallest, vertically placed line flower. Place this flower stem so that it extends downward slightly from the horizontal line extending from the rim of the container.

FIGURE 4–5   *Constructing a right-triangle design.*

(a) *Create the asymmetrical triangle outline with the skeleton flowers.*

Step 4: The flower to be placed at the left-side, horizontal position will only be approximately one-third the length of the tallest vertically placed line flower. Also slant this flower stem downward toward the base of the arrangement, if the stem holder will allow this treatment.

Step 5: Place a short-stemmed line flower at the front of the container, as described for the equilateral triangle design. Add the foliage at this point to form a background and to help fill in the central portion of the arrangement.

Step 6: The left-hand side of the right-triangle design must be purposely made heavier to balance the weight of the longer-stemmed flower that extends to the right side of the arrangement. Emphasize the main line of the triangle by placing line flowers along the left side of the axis and also along the horizontal line that extends to the right side of the design. The first flower added is approximately two-thirds to three-fourths the length of the tallest flower. Place it along the main axis and slightly to the right of the tallest flower.

Step 7: The next flower added is approximately one-half the length of the tallest flower. Place this flower to the left-hand side of the main axis so that a line extends from the tallest flower to the lowest flower on the left-hand side of the design.

Step 8: Repeat steps 6 and 7 along the horizontal axis, using the right-hand flower as a guide to stem lengths. The shorter stem will then extend downward toward the base of the container.

Step 9: Additional line flowers are required to complete the design. Place these in the central area of the design to provide harmony and unity.

Step 10: Add the mass and filler flowers to the arrangement starting near the top and sides and extending toward the center. Alternate the flowers and shorten the stems until the center is filled.

Step 11: Finish the arrangement by filling any loose holes in the design with foliage or filler flowers. The completed design will appear to have a right-triangular outline, without any flowers extending beyond the boundaries of this shape.

(b) Add the filler foliage and complete the triangle shape with spike flowers.

(c) Complete the design with the addition of the focal flowers and filler material.

Horizontal Design: The horizontal design makes an excellent centerpiece because it is attractive when viewed from either the front or the back. This design is arranged with a low profile so it will not block the view of seated dinner guests. The long and narrow shape of this style of arrangement repeats the long horizontal line of a rectangular table. This repetition of lines aids in establishing design unity.

The horizontal design is constructed in the same manner as a triangular arrangement, but with two notable changes. The height of the arrangement is reduced so that the horizontal length becomes one and one-half to two times the length of the container. The horizontal line appears best when the tips of the flowers placed in line with the container angle slightly downward. This gives the arrangement the appearance of being nearly like an inverted crescent design. Since this design style is viewed from both sides, it is arranged from both sides of the container. The skeleton flowers are placed midway between the back and front of the container. A focal point is then established on each side to create an accent within the design (see Figure 4–6).

This style of arrangement may be easily used with candles for an evening dinner party. When this is done, three candles may be placed in the arrangement. The center candle is tallest, with the two other candles placed on either side at the center line of the arrangement. All foliage and flowers located near the candles should be low enough so they will not be singed as the candles burn down. The horizontal centerpiece is constructed by the following methods:

FIGURE 4–6   *Constructing a horizontal arrangement.*

(a) Establish the low, horizontal triangle shape with the skeleton flowers.

(b) Create the outline and fill the center of the design with flowers.

(c) Complete the arrangement with the placement of filler flowers and focal flowers in the design.

Step 1: Since the horizontal arrangement is used primarily for tables where people will be seated, the design must necessarily exhibit a low profile. To create this low profile, select low containers having an oval or rectangular shape. The size of the container should be proportionate with the size of the table where it will be placed as a finished design. Floral foam stem holders are ideal for use in the containers, particularly when candles are to be included in the design. The top of the floral foam block should extend above the lip of the container

to a sufficient level to allow stems to be angled slightly downward along the horizontal axis of the arrangement.

Step 2: Place the skeleton flowers first in the container to establish the height and width relationship of the design. The flower stems to be placed along the horizontal axis will have a combined length of one and one-half to two times the length of the container. Place these at the sides along the center point of the container with their stem tips pointing slightly downward as they are inserted into the stem holder. The vertical flower height will equal approximately three-fourths to one times the length of the container. Also place it along the center line running through the container. When gladiolus or other one-sided spike flowers are used to create this vertical line, two individual spike tips may be required to provide florets on both the front and back sides of the arrangement. The placement of these gladiolus is done with one stem facing away from the other and on a shorter stem. When a candle is used as the vertical line, the line flowers at the top center position will not be required.

Step 3: Create a focal area on both the front and back sides of the design in the same manner as previously described for other triangular-shaped arrangements. Add foliage at this point to fill in the body of the container. Place foliage along the center line of the arrangement so it will be seen from both sides of the design while providing a background.

Step 4: Complete the design by placing the mass-type and filler flowers in the body of the arrangement. Add these to each side of the design so that they contribute to the arrangement from both sides. Those flowers that are clearly evident when viewed from either side of the design must be balanced, but not paired with those opposite them. Be careful to avoid placing flowers in exact pairs on either side of the vertical line extending through the center of the arrangement. These paired flowers will detract from the focal areas of the design.

Vertical Designs: The linear, vertical design is shaped to form a distinct line along the vertical axis of a container. These designs are best suited to situations where a strong vertical line is to be emphasized in a room decoration. These might be used in places where space is limiting and the height of the area is to be emphasized, such as in a narrow hallway, entryway, on a footed stand along a wall, or on a narrow table.

The vertical design is constructed in a tall, narrow container to emphasize the linear profile of this style (see Figure 4–7). These designs may be very tall, depending upon the type of plant materials and the containers being used. They will broaden slightly only at the focal area and may extend downward from the lip of the container, to continue the vertical line in both directions. The vertical arrangement style may be created as explained in the five steps detailed after Figure 4–7.

FIGURE 4–7   Constructing a vertical arrangement.

(a) Establish a strong vertical line using linear material.

(b) Fill the center of the design with foliage to conceal the support block and add the remaining linear flowers to create the vertical line.

(c) Complete the design with the addition of the focal flowers and filler material.

Step 1: Most vertical designs are created in tall, narrow containers so that their height will emphasize the strong lines of this design style. Some examples of containers that might be used include the large, antique milk cans or butter churns with dried flowers and grasses; ornate beer steins; or slender vases for fresh flowers. When these taller containers are used, the stem-holding device (preferably a floral foam product) should extend well above the lip of the container. When this is done, insert the plant materials so as to allow the lines to extend downward along the vertical axis of the container.

Low, shallow containers may be used to create the vertical design, also. Generally a needlepoint stem holder is used with this style of container for fresh flower designs. Because of the shape and depth of the rim of the container, the stem holder will not have to be elevated. Very dainty vertical designs may be created in these shallow containers, which may be displayed in narrow locations in any room setting.

Step 2: First establish the vertical line of the design. Place the tallest line flower stem in the center of the arrangement as far to the rear of the stem holder as is possible. Place the line flower stem that will extend downward from the focal area next. Position it so that it will extend downward from a point just above the rim of the container and push it into the floral foam at an upward slant. Insert this stem only deeply enough to anchor it, not allowing it to penetrate all the way through the foam.

Step 3: Emphasize the vertical line of the design by positioning additional line flowers along the vertical axis. Do not place these stems directly in front of the main flower stems; rather, stagger them by placing the tallest stem in the center of the container. Because the second stem is slightly shorter, place it to the right of the first flower. Because the third stem is shorter than the second, place it to the left of the first stem. Continue this pattern of stem placement from both the top and lower segments until the line is established.

Step 4: Linear foliage is often used to emphasize the vertical line of this design style. Once the primary flowers have established the main axis of the arrangement, the linear foliage may be included. Add the filler foliage sparingly to this design, since only the area surrounding the focal point will possess much depth of plant material. Add this foliage before establishing the focal area with flowers.

Step 5: Using the mass or form flowers to complete the vertical design, follow the linear outline established by the skeleton flowers. Also stagger these to form the vertical line, rather than creating a distinct line of flowers along the axis. Widen the focal area slightly by placing larger flowers in this region. However, avoid a triangular- or diamond-shaped silhouette.

CURVILINEAR DESIGNS

The soft, subtle lines of the curvilinear designs create a sophisticated formality when used in a room decoration. These lines lend a graceful restfulness to a design that imparts an elegant mood. The beginning floral designer should have mastered the techniques used in constructing the previous geometric design styles before attempting to create the curved designs. The designer who creates a curved-shaped arrangement must be skillful in achieving visual balance. This balance is needed to create a naturally free-flowing outline that has a formal appeal. Two styles of curvilinear designs are discussed in this chapter: *crescent* and *Hogarthian curve* (**S** curve).

Crescent Designs

The crescent design is constructed in a crescent-moon shape with a height at the left side that is two-thirds the length of the entire line of the arrangement. The curved foliage is placed to the side (usually left of the center) so that its tip nearly reaches the visual center line of the design. The focal point is located directly in line with the tip at the base of the arrangement. The arranger must be careful to balance the sizes of flowers as the curved line is established. The delicate line is maintained by using the smallest flowers at each point of the curve and the larger blooms at the center of interest. Flowers with a heavy visual weight are placed at the focal area to create balance in this design (Figure 4–8: *a, b, c*).

FIGURE 4–8   *Constructing a crescent design.*

(a) *Create the basic line of the arrangement with curved foliage.*

The seven steps to follow in constructing a crescent design are outlined on the next pages.

(b) Fill the center of the container with foliage to add depth to the arrangement and to conceal the support block.

Step 1: Select plant materials with a natural curve when creating a curvilinear style of design. Florists generally select foliages such as Scotch broom, eucalyptus, forsythia, and other easily curved materials for this purpose, when they are in season.

Curve the foliage branches by first rolling them firmly in the hands to form a tight coil. When the coil of foliage is released, the stems should assume a slightly curved form. Repeat this procedure several times if desired to obtain the proper degree of curvature to the stems. Then cut individual stem pieces from the main stem for use in the design.

Step 2: The crescent design will form a nearly circular pattern, as viewed from the front of the container. Many different container types are suitable for this style of arrangement, but a shallow, circular, or oval container is most functional. Either floral foam or needlepoint stem holders can be used to anchor the flowers and foliage.

Step 3: Place the curved foliage in the stem holder starting at the rear left corner and extending outward to the right front corner. The tallest stem at the rear left corner will be two-thirds the length of the completed crescent line of the arrangement. The tip of this curved foliage stem should nearly reach the center point of an imaginary circle formed by the curved line.

(c) Complete the design by placing the flowers along the lines of the curve and adding filler flowers.

The foliage stem that extends from the center of the focal area toward the right side will sweep gracefully upward to continue the circular line. The length of this right-hand element is approximately one-third the length of the completed crescent line or half the length of the tallest stem in the design.

Step 4: Insert the two curved foliage stems into the container to outline the crescent from the top left to the right side. Position additional curved stems in a staggered fashion to emphasize this curve on the left and right sides of the focal area. The left-hand side of the curve is emphasized to create balance. As the focal area is approached, the curve becomes widest. The foliage and flowers that are selected to form the curved line of the crescent design should be carried throughout the entire body of the arrangement to maintain unity.

Step 5: Next, fill the body of the arrangement sparingly with filler foliage (such as leatherleaf fern) to conceal the stem holder and provide depth to the design.

Step 6: Add the main flowers using the smallest buds at the tips of the crescent line and gradually increasing their sizes or visual weight as the focal area is approached. Place the focal flowers in the visual center of the design, which is in a line directly below the tip of the tallest curved foliage stem.

Occasionally, you may wish to form a curve using stiff-stemmed flowers. These may be made to form a moderate curve when wired with florist wire. Generally, this practice is avoided, since straight-stemmed flowers may be placed in a staggered line that conforms aesthetically to the general outline of the crescent design.

Step 7: When completed, the crescent design will have an obvious void of flowers and foliage in the upper-right-hand quadrant of the arrangement. The designer should avoid the temptation to fill this open area with foliage or flowers. A customary mistake made by novice designers is to place flowers in this area, much the same as is done with the circular design, as if it were to be viewed from above.

Hogarthian Curve (S Curve)

The Hogarthian curve is a sophisticated asymmetrical design named after the English artist, William Hogarth (1697–1764). This design has a graceful appearance that lends formality to a room decor (see Figure 4–9). The Hogarthian curve design has the outline of an **S**, hence its nickname.

FIGURE 4–9 *A Hogarthian curve (S curve) design.*

This can be an elegant design when used for very formal gatherings or in ornate stemmed containers. Florists design this arrangement style infrequently, because its function is limited to rather precise occasions. The principal steps in constructing a Hogarthian curve are as follows:

Step 1: Use tall, stemmed compotes or raised containers for this design because a portion of the floral line extends below the rim of the container.

Step 2: Construct the **S** outline in exactly the same manner as the crescent design, with the exception that the line is reversed on one side of the focal point. The **S** shape is separated into two elements, with the upper curve consisting of two-thirds the height of the total design. The lower portion of the curve may be constructed with either curved material or dainty, dangling flowers. The focal point is often depicted (particularly in permanent designs) by a cluster of grapes gracefully dangling over the rim of the container.

DESIGN GUIDELINES FOR BEGINNERS

1. Keep the balance and proportion of each design in the proper perspective. The overall height of the arrangement is usually between one and one-half to two times the height or width of the container, depending on the style of design to be created. Use these measurements as a guide only when establishing the skeleton of the design.

2. Before you begin construction, know what size and shape your arrangement will have upon completion. Having a general idea of the size and shape of the finished design will prevent the necessity of reconstructing the arrangement several times to achieve balance. Floral foams, when used, will disintegrate with repeated reinsertion of stems.

3. Work quickly and precisely when constructing an arrangement. Flowers soon wilt when left out of water. Be certain that the floral foam and container are amply filled with preservative-water before adding the flowers.

4. The focal point, when present, should be clearly apparent; yet it should not be created by a massing of closely spaced flowers. This technique would give the effect of a circle drawn around the center of the design. Carefully placed flowers having a larger size or strong contrast will be most effective in creating a center of interest.

5. When flowers of the same size, color, texture, or form are used in creating an arrangement, it is best to use an odd number of blooms. The flower numbers are apparent up to nine blooms. Odd numbers of flowers (1, 3, 5, 7, or 9) are more pleasing to the eye and aid in avoiding complete symmetry in designs.

6. Place flowers so space is allowed between each bloom. Generally, the petals from one flower should not touch those of another. Insert foliage in these spaces between the flowers.

7. As they are found in the wild, flowers do not all grow at the same height or in straight lines. When creating line or rhythm in a design, avoid placing flowers in lines or rows. A staggered row or line will create the desired effect without allowing flowers to be placed at the same exact heights. A vertical staggered line is constructed by placing a flower slightly below and to the right of the first. The third flower is then placed slightly below the second and on the left side of the first. This pattern is continued throughout the design until the desired effect is created.

8. Create unity and harmony in your designs by using each color, texture, or flower type throughout the entire arrangement. Use smaller blooms at the outside perimeters of the arrangement and larger ones toward the center. A lack of unity exists when one type of flower is used to form the skeleton or backbone of an arrangement and the center of the design contains another.

9. A successful design will have three dimensions. This is created by constructing each arrangement from the back of the container toward the front (for one-sided designs). When properly located, the focal flower (accent) will be the most prominent and placed in front of all other primary flowers in the arrangement.

10. Place foliage in such a manner as to give a natural appearance to a design. Foliage placed between, and extending through, the flowers will soften the arrangement. Also use the foliage to conceal the stems and holder at the base of the container. Keep in mind that the foliage used in florists' arrangements is often as expensive as the flowers. Even the small and broken branches or leaves may be used in completing the arrangement.

11. Finish the back of all one-sided arrangements. Even though the arrangement is intended to be viewed only from one side, adding foliage or a few left-over flowers will conceal the flower stems and stem holder at the rear. This is the final step for a conscientious designer who takes pride in his or her work.

12. Once you have mastered the skills required in constructing the arrangement styles described in this chapter, you are prepared to attempt the more advanced designs. Often advanced designers do not follow the general design rules explicitly, but are able to create arrangements that are subtly attractive and appealing. These designers have reached the highest level of the profession.

SELECTED REFERENCES

BENZ, M. *Flowers: Geometric Form,* 3rd ed. Houston, Tex.: San Jacinto Publishing Company, 1966.

CUTLER, K. N. *How to Arrange Flowers for all Occasions.* Garden City, N.Y.: Doubleday & Company, 1967.

FORT, V. P. *A Complete Guide to Flower Arrangement.* New York: Viking Press, 1962.

GORDON, R. L. *Professional Flower Arranging for Beginners.* New York: Arco Publishing Company, 1974.

HAWKES, F. A. *The Gracious Art of Flower Arrangement.* Garden City, N.Y.: Doubleday & Company, 1969.

HILLIER, F. B. *Basic Guide to Flower Arranging.* New York: McGraw-Hill Book Company, 1974.

McDANIEL, G. L. *Ornamental Horticulture.* Reston, Va.: Reston Publishing Company, 1979.

ROCKWELL, F. F., and E. C. GRAYSON. *The Rockwell's New Complete Book of Flower Arrangement.* Garden City, N.Y.: Doubleday & Company, 1960.

STRATMAN, T. S. *Retail Floriculture, Book II: Designing and Care of Flowers and Foliage.* Ohio Agricultural Education Curriculum Materials Service. Columbus: Ohio State University, 1976.

TERMS TO KNOW

Asymmetrical	Radiating	Symmetrical
Horizontal	Skeleton flowers	Vertical

STUDY QUESTIONS

1. Discuss how each of the various floral design shapes may be used in decorating for best display.
2. Make a list of the basic materials needed by the floral designer for constructing the arrangements described in this chapter.
3. List some typical flowers generally used in constructing each of the geometric designs described in this chapter.
4. Discuss how negative space is used in asymmetrical designs.
5. Pick one of the basic designs and discuss how the principles and elements of design are used to create the arrangement.
6. What criteria are used in selecting the appropriate container for an arrangement?

SUGGESTED ACTIVITIES

1. Make a poster showing each of the geometric designs for display in the classroom.
2. Make a notebook of pictures cut from magazines showing the use of floral designs in home settings.
3. Invite a retail florist to demonstrate the various techniques used in cut-flower arranging.
4. Using the pictures of flower arrangements collected from various magazines, conduct a class discussion about their design features. Show why some features may be good or poor, based upon the principles and elements of floral design.
5. Construct a circular arrangement using:
   8 stems of leatherleaf fern   1–2 stems of Gypsophila
   2–3 stems of pompon chrysanthemums
6. Create an equilateral triangular design using the following:
   8 stems of leatherleaf fern   1 stem of statice (if available)
   6 stems of gladiolus   2 stems of pompon chrysanthemums
7. Make a crescent or a Hogarthian curve in the appropriate container using the following plant materials in the quantities needed:
   eucalyptus or Scotch broom   leatherleaf fern
   roses or pixie carnations   filler flower (your choice)
   (use an odd number)

CHAPTER 5:

Corsage Construction

Corsages are still very popular florists' items for special occasions. Florists sell corsages mainly for special dances such as formals and proms. Corsages are also sold extensively during the Christmas, Easter, and Mother's Day holidays. One of the more important uses for corsages, however, is for weddings. Beginning floral designers will find corsage construction exciting and fun as they learn to create new styles. The techniques of corsage construction are not difficult to master, but will require a high degree of manual dexterity on the part of the designer. These skills are useful for both the professional florist and the home flower arranger.

DESIGN GUIDELINES FOR CORSAGES

The construction of florists' corsages resembles the arrangement of flowers in containers. The bow and trim become an integral part of the design and satin leaves may provide the foliage. The principles and elements already discussed for cut-flower arrangements still apply. However, a few additional principles must be followed when constructing corsages.

Scale: The size and form of the corsage should be proportional with the wearer. A tiny girl might not feel comfortable wearing a large Cattleya orchid corsage.

Emphasis: The center of interest of a corsage is created at the point where the flower stems meet. This is most often the location where the largest bloom or the bow is placed.

Balance: The corsage must be constructed so as to be easy to wear. Smaller flowers are placed at the top and edges, with the focal area given the most visual weight. Normally the flowers will extend through the accent area and will be located in a balanced fashion on both sides of the center of interest. It is not considered good design to place flowers at one end of the corsage with the bow placed at the bottom. However, this practice may not be avoided with some corsage design styles. A well-designed corsage should appear as an accessory to the dress or gown on which it is worn. The presence of the corsage should be apparent but not stand out unnecessarily.

Construction: The corsage must be constructed securely enough to retain its original design. This should be done with a minimum of wires and floral tape to avoid large masses of stems at the base. Flowers should be positioned for best effect and firmness in construction. The designer learns to position flowers in a corsage so that they will not appear as a tight mass of blooms or as a loose mixture of petals and wired stems. When the wired stems are placed together while styling the corsage, the wires are taped together rather than twisted. This practice eliminates the thick masses of wire in the center of the corsage that create an unnatural appearance.

Design: The corsage designer should create floral pieces that will be compatible with the intended use. A corsage that is intended for a formal dance, for example, should be constructed with more style, using more elegant flowers and high-quality background materials and ribbon.

Flower colors should be coordinated with the dress, the complexion and hair color of the wearer, and the lighting available (for day or evening occasions). For example, a blonde-complexioned girl will be best complemented by a yellow corsage. Whenever the corsage colors may be selected for a specific gown or dress, a related flower hue should be chosen. Often the designer must construct a corsage without knowing the color of the dress on which it will be worn. Generally, florists will select a white corsage color for these situations, since white flowers or ribbon are considered appropriate for nearly all occasions. When constructing corsages to be worn on the shoulder, the flowers should be placed in the corsage to be worn as they grow, pointing upward.

PREPARATION OF MATERIALS USED IN CORSAGES

Wiring Corsage Flowers

Wires and floral tape replace the flower stems in a well-constructed design. Eliminating the natural stems in corsage designs is done to create a sturdy, less bulky framework. Corsage flowers are also placed on wire stems to make them easier to handle and to keep the flowers in position when worn.

The wires used for this purpose are green-enameled sections in lengths of 6 to 12 inches. Enameled wire is used to prevent rust formation and staining on clothing. The narrower gauges (nos. 24 to 32) are generally selected for this purpose to reduce the bulkiness of the corsage.

Corsage flowers and foliages are wired by different methods, depending on their size, form, and intended use. These wiring techniques include the Hook, the Insertion, the Hairpin, and the Wrapped-Wire methods.

Hook Method: The hook method (often called *shepherd crook* method) of wiring is used to secure blooms having a flattened head or crown and those without a thickened calyx region. Daisies, chrysanthemums, and asters are examples of flowers that may be wired to form stems in this fashion. The natural stem is removed below the calyx, leaving a stub that is approximately ¼ to ½ inch in length. A mediumweight wire is inserted through the base of the flower near the original stem. The wire is extended beyond the center of the bloom for a short distance (see Figure 5–1). A hook or U-shaped bend is placed on the end of the wire before being pulled back snugly into the center of the petals. The designer must be very careful when pulling the wire hook back into the petals or the flower head may be split apart. This wired stem may then be wrapped with floral tape.

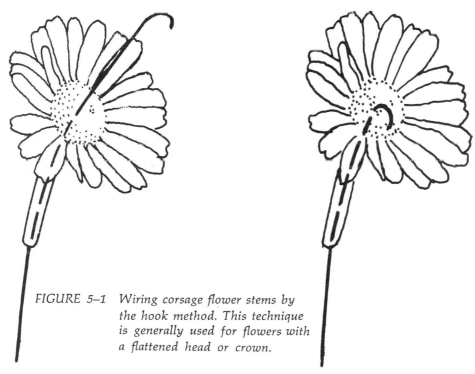

FIGURE 5–1 *Wiring corsage flower stems by the hook method. This technique is generally used for flowers with a flattened head or crown.*

Insertion Method: Flowers with a mass-type head (large, thickened calyx) may be wired by the insertion method. Examples of flowers that may be wired effectively by this method include roses, carnations, and large-flowered orchids. The original flower stem is removed at a point

FIGURE 5–2   *Wiring corsage flower stems by the insertion method. This technique is used for flowers having a mass-type head (large, thickened calyx cup).*

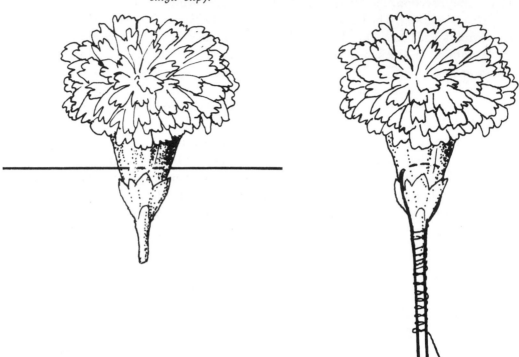

immediately below the calyx of the bloom. A heavier wire (nos. 22–24 gauge) is inserted through the calyx midway from the base to the petal so that equal lengths of wire protrude from each side (see Figure 5–2). This wire is bent to form a stem with both ends of the wire pulled together at the base of the calyx. A thin-diameter corsage wire (nos. 26–32 gauge) is twisted around the calyx and original wire before the entire length is wrapped in floral tape.

Wrapped-Wire Method: Delicate flowers that will remain on their original stem and some foliages used in corsage work are wired by the wrapped-wire method. A thin-diameter wire is laid along the length of the stem to be supported so that an equal length of wire remains above and below the area to be wrapped. The upper portion of the wire is twisted around the wire that extends below the stem (see Figure 5–3). When it is possible to do so, the wire should be looped around a leaf petiole or stem branch to provide added security. The stem is completed by wrapping the wire with floral tape (*above left, next page*).

FIGURE 5–3
Wiring flower stems by the wrapped-wire method.

FIGURE 5–4
Wiring corsage flower stems by the hairpin method.

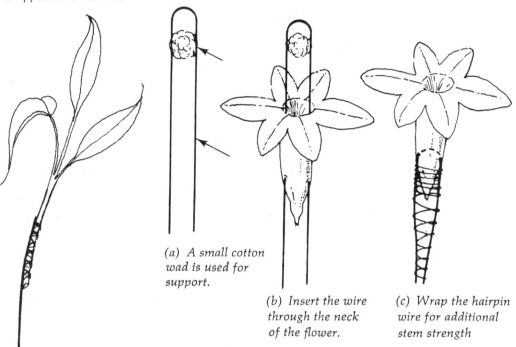

(a) *A small cotton wad is used for support.*

(b) *Insert the wire through the neck of the flower.*

(c) *Wrap the hairpin wire for additional stem strength*

Hairpin Method: Tube-shaped flowers (such as tuberoses and stephanotis) are supported by folding a lightweight wire (nos. 28–30 gauge) into the shape of a narrow hairpin (see Figure 5–4). A small wad of cotton is included in the center of the hairpin wire to lend support and protect the fragile petals. This wire is inserted through the neck of the tubular bloom from the face of the flower. A second lightweight wire is wrapped around the base of the flower and the extended lengths of wire created by the hairpin. The stem is completed by wrapping the wires with floral tape.

Corsage Tapes

The wired stems on corsage flowers are not attractive unless covered by floral tape. Floral tapes are available in widths of ¼, ½, or 1 inch and in many different colors. Florists generally use the narrower widths of tape in green, white, orchid, and brown colors for corsage work. These floral tapes are marketed under such names as Floratape® and Parafilm®. White floral tape is used on most wedding bouquets and corsages. Green tape is generally used for rose corsages, boutonnieres, and any design work where

FIGURE 5–5   *Wrapping the wired stem with floral tape; stretch the tape tightly for best results.*

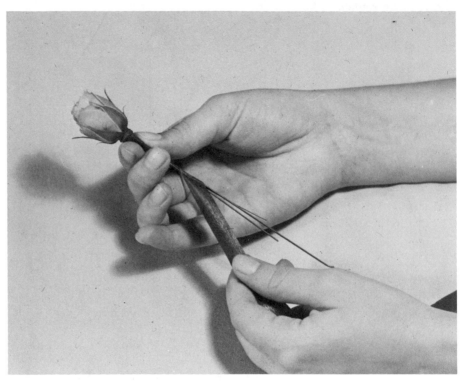

green-colored stems are desired. Orchid-colored tape is used most often for wrapping the stems of lavender Cattleya orchids and brown tape for Cymbidium orchids or dried flowers in fall colors.

Flower stems are wrapped with floral tapes by placing the material near the flower head from behind. The flower stem is held in one hand and twirled as the tape is being guided by the other (see Figure 5–5). The twirling action feeds the tape onto the stem as the opposite hand guides the tape placement and stretches it tightly around the stem. After a little practice, the stems may be rapidly and smoothly wrapped with floral tape.

Corsage Accessories

The natural foliage of flowers most often used in corsages and wedding designs does not remain as fresh as do the flowers for extended periods of time out of water. For this reason, artificial foliages are selected by the florist to add a fuller appearance to the designs. The accessories are added to enhance, and sometimes substitute for, the living flowers and foliages when a corsage or wedding bouquet is being created.

Artificial Leaves: Substitute foliage (glamor leaves) may be used by florists to add the appearance of natural greenery to a corsage. Most leaves are taped together in sprays of five or more stems that may be used together or split apart into individual leaves for placement in corsages. Most florists prefer to divide the stems into individual leaves for better placement in corsage work.

Satin leaves may be constructed by the designer from strips of ribbon. Select ribbon that is 1½ inches or larger in width. The satin ribbon is cut into lengths that are twice its width. The two opposite corners are folded downward to meet at the bottom center of the strip of ribbon. This triangular piece of ribbon is doubled over on itself, leaving the smooth-finished side of the ribbon on the inner fold. The bottom of each side of the triangular pieces of ribbon is gathered (bunched) from the center to the tip. The entire ribbon is placed on a wire stem and wrapped with floral tape (see Figure 5-6). These satin leaves may be varied in size for use in corsages and other floral pieces.

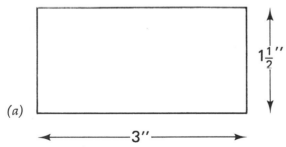

(a)

FIGURE 5-6 *Constructing satin leaves. (a) Cut satin ribbon twice as long as the width. (b) Fold the top corners into the center and gather at the base. (c) Use a wire to create a stem. (d) Wrap the stem with floral tape to complete the satin leaf.*

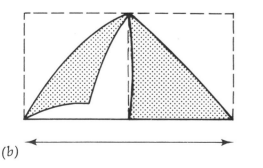

(b)   *(c)*   *(d)*

FIGURE 5–7   Net corsage accessories. (a) Net wired in a butterfly shape.

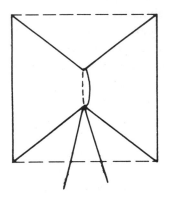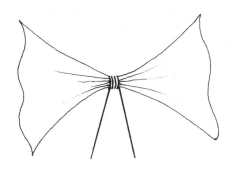

(a) Net wired in a butterfly shape.

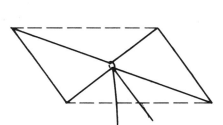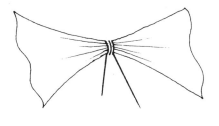

(b) Rectangular net wired in a fan shape.

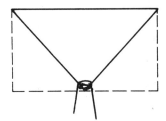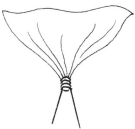

(c) Net folded and wired to create a tuft.

Net and Lace Trims: Net background material is added to a corsage or wedding bouquet to create a fullness in a design without adding weight. Net materials available for florist design work are sold in different patterns and styles, known as tulle, net, and Lacelon®. These are available in widths ranging in size from 2⅞ to 8 inches, with the 2⅞ inch (no. 40) and 4½ inch (no. 120) widths used most often in corsage work or wedding bouquets. For formal corsages and wedding work, the finest lace and net should be used.

The net materials may be cut into lengths equal to their width to create either a net *butterfly, fan,* or *tuft.* The net butterfly is constructed from net with a slanted cut at the ends. The net strip is gathered into the center and wired onto a stem of no. 28 or no. 30 gauge wire. The fan is constructed by first cutting a square section of net. This is gathered at the bottom and wired to create a fan-shaped piece of net on an artificial stem. The net tuft is constructed in a similar manner to the butterfly, except that the material is drawn to the center and formed into a circle before the wire stem is added. Each of these net accessories is finished by wrapping the wired stem with floral tape (see Figure 5–7).

The net materials may be added to a corsage to provide background (fan) or in place of foliage or flowers as a filler (butterfly or tuft). The corsage may be constructed with alternate patterns of flowers and net as the design takes shape. Larger wedding bouquets and nosegays may be constructed by first forming a net pillow or puff in the center of the design. Flowers are then added to the bouquet among the tufts and folds of the net to create a beautiful, yet simply designed arrangement.

Ribbon and Bows: Ribbon is made into bows or streamers for corsages and wedding bouquets, as well as for cut flower designs in containers. Ribbon styles vary considerably according to the fashion trends. Satin ribbon remains popular for an elegant addition to any design. Ribbon is available in bolt widths ranging from ¼ inch to 4½ inches (Figure 5–8).

FIGURE 5–8 *Ribbon widths with corresponding number designations.*

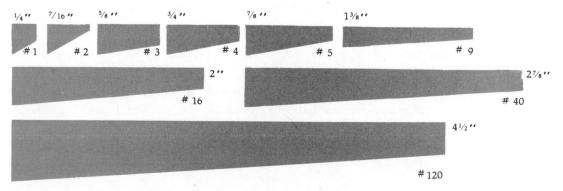

Corsage bows are constructed from ribbon having a width measurement of ¼ inch (no. 1), 7/16 inch (no. 2), or ⅝ inch (no. 3). Satin ribbon and metalline (spray ribbon) are used in widths of 2⅞ inches (no. 40) and 4½ inches (no. 120) for bouquets or funeral sprays. A popular-sized ribbon for use in decorating flowering plants, cut-flower arrangements or bouquets, and other decorating purposes has a width measurement of 1⅜ inches (no. 9).

Corsage bows should be constructed in proportion to the size of the design. The streamers and bow loops must not attract attention away from the flowers. Placing the bow in relation to the flowers creates the focal point of the corsage. The bow is often located at the base of the corsage, since its original purpose was to bind the stems during construction. Today, the location of the bow is not limited to this area, since wires and tape serve to hold the stems together. Regardless of the style of corsage being created, the primary flowers should be directed upward, just as they grow.

Regardless of the size of ribbon used or intended use of the bow, the construction is the same (see Figure 5–9). Most satin ribbons are single-faced or smooth on only one side. The loops appear best when the smooth side is always on top of the bow. Constructing a florist bow is quite simple when the following steps are used:

Step 1: First hold the ribbon in the left hand (for right-handed persons) so that the smooth side faces you. The short end of the ribbon should extend about 2–3 inches below your left thumb. If a larger bow is being constructed or a longer streamer is desired, the tail may be made proportionately longer.

FIGURE 5–9   *Constructing a bow.*

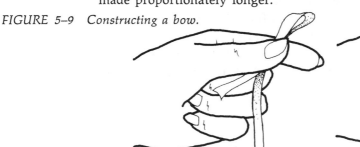

(a) *Establish the size of the bow when you make the first loop.*   (b) *Reverse the ribbon as you work to show the smooth side.*

Step 2: Form a loop above your thumb of equal length as the lower streamer (or one-half the width of the finished bow). Do this by bringing the ribbon back to your thumb and joining the two together between the thumb and forefinger. Press the loop firmly between the thumb and forefinger to reduce the bulkiness of the bow in the center.

Step 3: Form the first lower loop in the same manner. However, reverse the ribbon to bring the smooth side of the ribbon to the top of the bow before forming the loop. This is required only when one-sided ribbon is being used.

Step 4: Complete the second pair of loops (one above and one below the center) in a similar manner. Reverse the ribbon before forming each new loop. After completing each loop, press the ribbon firmly between the left thumb and forefinger.

Step 5: Once two pairs of loops are completed, add a small loop at the center of the bow to conceal the anchor wire that will be added later. Form this small loop in exactly the same manner as the others, except that it will be only about 1 inch in length (corsage bows) and is formed by simply rolling the ribbon over the thumb.

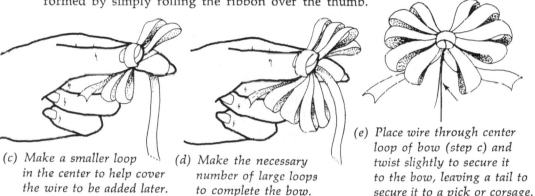

(c) Make a smaller loop in the center to help cover the wire to be added later. *(d) Make the necessary number of large loops to complete the bow.* *(e) Place wire through center loop of bow (step c) and twist slightly to secure it to the bow, leaving a tail to secure it to a pick or corsage.*

Step 6: Add two more loops leaving a streamer (tail) at the end of the bow before cutting the ribbon. The streamer that remains should extend to the same side of the bow as the one that was first formed. Most corsage bows will consist of three pair of loops (three above and three below the center) plus the small loop at the center. The number of loops formed will depend upon the size of ribbon, bow size, and the degree of fullness desired in the finished bow. The accepted practice is to form an odd number of pair loops whenever constructing a bow.

Step 7: Anchor the bow by running a no. 28 or 30 wire through the smallest loop and around to the back of the bow. Equal lengths of the wire should extend backward from the bow. Secure the wire by twisting the two lengths of wire firmly at the back of the bow leaving ample wire to be tied to the corsage. (*Note:* Tying the bow loops with a length of ribbon instead of a wire is not recommended. The knots so formed plus any you need to tie the bow to the corsage would create a cumbersome mass of ribbon at the base of a corsage.)

DESIGNING CORSAGES

Corsage designs are similar to cut-flower arrangements in containers, except that they are designed to be worn or carried. Although most corsages contain a bow, this addition is not always necessary to finish a design. Construction of corsages begins with wiring flowers and preparing accessory materials. These topics have been discussed earlier under "Preparation of Materials used in Corsages." Florists design corages in many styles and from a large array of floral materials. The basic corsage styles and more typical flowers used will be discussed here. The more common styles for florists' corsages include the *shoulder corsage* and the *wrist corsage*.

Shoulder Corsages

A shoulder corsage is normally designed in a crescent shape to be worn by women on the left side (or sometimes on the right or around the front collar). The basic pattern of these corsages appears as either a crescent or a triangle that has been reduced in size, although other geometric shapes may also be found. The smallest buds are placed at the top (and sometimes also at the bottom) of the corsage. Several types of shoulder corsage styles may be created easily by the beginning student. These will be described in detail, with outlines of each step used in their construction.

SINGLE-CARNATION CORSAGE

Procedure:

Step 1: Remove the natural stem from a standard carnation. Replace this with a chenille (pipe cleaner) stem by inserting it into the base of the calyx at the point of attachment with the original stem. Wrap the base of the calyx and chenille stem with the floral tape. (*Note:* The original stem may be replaced with wires rather than with a chenille stem, if desired. Use the crossed-wire insertion method for wiring the carnation flower.)

Step 2: Place a net fan background behind the carnation flower. Wrap the wired stems tightly with floral tape. (*Note:* Less formal corsages may be backed with foliage such as leatherleaf or camellia instead of using the net materials.)

Step 3: Add the bow to the base of the flower by wrapping the two wire ends around the corsage stem. Do this by twisting the wires together firmly. Cut the remaining wire.

Step 4: Finish the corsage by removing all unwanted wire or stems. Tape all cut ends and cover the wires that secure the bow with tape also. Arrange the bow loops for best appearance (see Figure 5–10).

FIGURE 5–10 *A single-carnation corsage. This simple corsage requires one standard carnation. It is quick to construct and is often used when large numbers of corsages are required.*

FIGURE 5–11 *A carnation boutonniere.*

BOUTONNIERE

The boutonniere is designed to be worn on the buttonhole of a man's lapel. Most boutonnieres resemble a single-flower corsage in construction. However, since this design is to be worn by a man, it should not be too ornate. There are several types of boutonniere styles, but most consist of only a single flower placed on an artificial stem (see Figure 5–11).

Procedure:

Step 1: Stem a rose, carnation, or any other appropriate single flower as previously described.

Step 2: Tape the stem with green floral tape.

Step 3: Bend the stem into a small, flattened circle at the base. (An alternate method is to leave the taped stem straight, but shortened.) Add a boutonniere pin by inserting the point into the base of the calyx.

If desired, a small leaf from leatherleaf fern or other appropriate foliage may be added as background for more formal occasions. No net or ribbon is included in a boutonniere.

DOUBLE-CARNATION CORSAGE

The double-carnation corsage is not a well-designed arrangement. The purpose of this style is to provide a corsage that may be mass produced and can be worn in either direction without appearing to be upside-down (see Figure 5–12).

FIGURE 5–12   *A double-carnation corsage. This simple corsage is constructed with two standard carnations wired together and a bow placed between the flowers.*

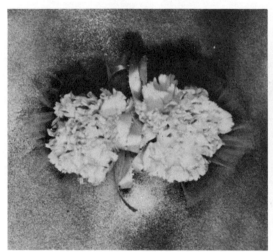

FIGURE 5–13   *A wire frame may be constructed before the flowers are added to aid in making double-carnation corsages more rapidly during busy periods.*

Procedure:

Step 1: Stem two flowers of equal size as previously described.

Step 2: Place a net fan behind each bloom. Leaves may be substituted for net when less formal corsages are desired.

Step 3: Join the two individual corsages at the center with wire and tape.

Step 4: Add a bow between the blooms and tape all work to be concealed. Add an appropriate corsage pin. (*Note:* A preconstructed frame may be created beforehand to reduce the labor required during the busy corsage holidays. A chenille frame may be used for this design style, with the flowers inserted at each end of the frame [see Figure 5–13].)

FIGURE 5–14
A corsage constructed from miniature (pixie) carnation flowers.

FEATHERED-CARNATION CORSAGE

The standard carnation bloom is often too large and bulky for proper corsage construction. The floral designer may wish to split the larger bloom into several smaller portions to be worked into a well-styled corsage. Although many florists are now replacing feathered carnations with miniature (pixie) carnations (Figure 5–14), this technique may be used in various styles of corsage construction. Feathered carnations are especially suitable in designs when mixed with sweetheart roses. The carnation flower is feathered in the following manner (see Figure 5–15):

Procedure:

Step 1: Remove the carnation flower from its natural stem at the point where the calyx is attached.

Step 2: While holding the flower head by the base of the calyx, press firmly with the thumb and forefinger until the pistil of the flower slips free and can be removed.

Step 3: Peel the calyx away from the petals (much like peeling a banana). This leaves the florets free, yet still attached at the base.

FIGURE 5–15   Feathering a standard carnation flower to create several smaller blooms. (a) Peel the calyx to expose the attached florets.

(b) Wrap a fine wire tightly around the bases of the divided floret pieces without cutting the petals.

(c) Secure the florets to the wired stem with tightly wrapped floral tape.

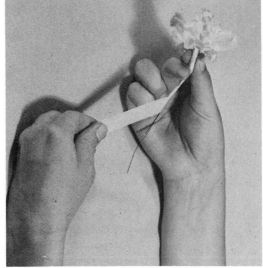

Step 4: Divide the florets into five or possibly six sections. Allow the sizes of these sections to vary. Loose petals may be placed together to form an individual floret.

Step 5: Place a 6-inch length of no. 30 florist wire an equal distance from the base of the florets.

Step 6: Wrap the wire tightly (but avoid cutting through the florets) from the base of the florets to a point near the top that will form a firm flower head. Wind the tail of the wire back down the stem to the lower wire, which forms the stem. Two windings of the wire around the floret near the top of the thumb should be sufficient for this procedure.

Step 7: Tape each wired stem firmly to conceal the wire and add support to the florets. (*Note:* Be certain that the tape is stretched tightly and extends high enough to prevent the flopping or spilling of florets.)

BASIC CORSAGE CONSTRUCTION

Constructing a simplified corsage style will be described next. A variation in this style is also shown for corsages which may include sweetheart roses, feathered carnations, miniature (pixie) carnations, or daisy chrysanthemums.

Sweetheart Roses and Feathered Carnations
Materials Needed:

- 4–5 feathered carnation florets (pink), wired and taped
- 3 pink net fans, wired and taped
- 3–4 pink net tufts, wired and taped
- 3 pink glamor leaves on stems
- 3 pink sweetheart rose buds, wired and taped
- 1 pink corsage bow
- White floral tape, wire scissors, 1 corsage pin
- Decorative bee, butterfly, or other accessory (optional)

Procedure:

Step 1: Place a single glamor leaf stem in the left hand. Behind this leaf add a net fan. Allow the leaf to extend above the fan (Figure 5–16).

Step 2: Place the smallest sweetheart rose bud above the leaf and net fan. The leaf tip should extend about 1 inch above the flower. Tape these stems together. Avoid wrapping the wires around each other since the sticky tape will hold the stems securely.

FIGURE 5–16 *Constructing a corsage with sweetheart roses and feathered carnations. (a) Begin the corsage by taping together a net fan or butterfly, glamor leaf, and a small rose bud. (b) Place a carnation floret below the rose to the right and another to the left side. (c) Add net to the left and right sides along with a second rose bud and glamor leaf. (d) Add additional carnation florets to the left and right sides with net and a third glamor leaf.*

Step 3: Place the smallest carnation floret to the right and slightly below the rose bud. Then place a second carnation floret below the first floret and to the left in a manner similar to arranging cut flowers in a container. Tape these stems.

*... THEN (e) Place the third rose bud as a focal flower with additional net
and a carnation floret. (f) Complete the corsage by adding a
bow and cutting off and taping the wire stem.*

Step 4: Place a net tuft between the first two carnation florets. Place a
second net fan behind the left side of the corsage. Then place the
second rose bud to the right side of the center in the corsage. Then
tape these stems.

Step 5: Place a net tuft to the left of the last rose bud added. Add a carnation floret to the left of this net tuft and slightly below the rose
bud. Add a second glamor leaf stem to the right side of the corsage
next to the last rose bud. Then tape these stems.

Step 6: Place a net fan along the right side of the corsage behind the
glamor leaf stem. Place a carnation floret above the fan. Place a net
tuft to the left side of this floret. Then place the third glamor leaf
stem and a carnation floret along the left side of the corsage as you
work toward the base. Tape these stems securely.

Step 7: Place the third and largest rose bud in the center of the corsage.
Then place the remaining net tufts and carnation florets around the
rose to fill the spaces. Then tape these stems.

Step 8: Once the size and shape of the corsage is completed, add the bow.
Attach this to the base of the stem. If an accessory is to be added,
place it near the largest rose bud at the base of the design and before
attaching the bow.

Step 9: Also add the bow to the side of the corsage, giving the design a
crescent-shaped outline. Tape all wires and cut ends of stems to
finish the corsage. Place the corsage pin in the finished design.

Rose Corsage with Camellia Leaves
Materials Needed:

- 5 camellia leaves, stemmed and taped
- 4–5 net tufts (pink), stemmed and taped
- 7 pink sweetheart roses, stemmed and taped
- Roll of green floral tape (all stems to be in green tape)
- 1 pink corsage bow
- Wire scissors, corsage pin

FIGURE 5–17 *Constructing a rose corsage. (a) Begin the corsage by taping together a background leaf, net accessory, and a small rose bud. (b) Establish the shape of the corsage by adding the roses, net, and background leaves. (c) Complete the rose corsage by adding a bow and finishing the wired stem.*

Procedure:

Step 1: Place a stemmed camellia leaf in the left hand. Behind this leaf add a net tuft.

Step 2: Place the smallest sweetheart rose bud above the leaf. The leaf will extend slightly above the flower. Tape these stems securely.

Step 3: Place a second bloom to the right and below the first. Place a third bloom below the second and to the left side to stagger the line. Separate the flowers with net tufts and add leaves as the corsage is formed. This process of alternating the flowers and net tufts continues until the shape of the corsage is established.

Step 4: Tape the main stem after adding every third or fourth wired stem. Add the leaves and net in appropriate locations in the corsage to provide form and to fill spaces.

Step 5: Either add the bow at the bottom or arrange it along the left side of the corsage. Remove the excess wires and corsage stem. Then tape the cut ends to conceal them and to protect the wearer's clothing. Add a 2-inch corsage pin to complete the design (see Figure 5–17).

ORCHID CORSAGES

The Cattleya orchid is the largest of the orchid types used by florists for corsages. Because of its size, it is generally used alone to create a corsage. Constructing an orchid corsage is similar to the other designs, except that fewer flowers are used. Wiring orchids is also rather specific since these are very fragile flowers. The Cattleya orchid corsage is constructed using the following steps (see Figure 5–18):

FIGURE 5–18   *Constructing a Cattleya orchid corsage. (a) Place the orchid stem on a water tube or wire with a moistened tissue.*

Step 1: The Cattleya orchid requires two wires, a heavy one to strengthen and extend the stem and a smaller wire to anchor the flower onto the stem.

Step 2: Insert the heavy wire (no. 22 or no. 24) through the short stem just below the petals of the orchid. This wire provides strength and holds the flower in the proper position.

Step 3: Insert a smaller wire (no. 28 or no. 30) through the base of the flower at a right angle to the stem. Wrap this wire around the stem and the larger wire and then lay it flat along the stem. Also provide a method for adding water to the end of the stem. Place either a half-filled water tube or a piece of dampened cotton (or tissue) over the cut end of the stem. Hold it in place with the lighter wire strand as you wrap it over the stem.

Step 4: Then wrap the wired stem with floral tape, including the water tube or cotton, to provide strength and form a natural-appearing stem. The stem should taper to the base. This can be accomplished by proper taping and removal of bulky wires.

FIGURE 5–18   (continued)
              (b) Add net behind the petals.

AND (c) Complete the corsage by adding a bow, cutting and taping the wire stem, and curling the stem behind the corsage.

Step 5: Place three pieces of net fan or butterfly strategically behind the orchid petals to provide a softened background. Many florists also include three looped pieces of metallic cord to add strength and protection for the fragile petals. Tape these stems to form a solid stem for the corsage.

Step 6: Add the bow below the lip of the orchid. Tape this across the back to prevent the wearer from being stuck by any cut wire ends.

Step 7: Cut the stem of the corsage to an appropriate length below the bow. Then tape and gently curl it to provide a place to pin the corsage to a dress. Include a corsage pin on the stem to complete the corsage.

The Cymbidium orchid is even more popular as a corsage flower than the Cattleya. Cymbidium orchids are wired in the same fashion, but are often combined into a corsage by using two blooms with a bow at the base (see Figure 5–19).

FIGURE 5–19   *A double Cymbidium orchid corsage.*

Phalaenopsis and Vanda orchids are quite fragile blooms that require specific support when used in corsages or wedding work. Corsages constructed from either of these orchids are handled in the following manner:

Step 1: Tape a 6-inch length of no. 26 or no. 28 wire tightly and smoothly. Bend this to form a hook with a slight crook at the top.

Step 2: Insert the hooked wire carefully from above the orchid lip and down the sides of the petals. The wire does not puncture any part of the flower; rather, it provides a base for supporting the bloom.

Step 3: Place a piece of dampened cotton or a water tube over the cut end of the flower stem and hold it in place with a length of no. 26 wire. Tape the entire stem, including the tube or cotton, to provide a natural appearing stem.

Step 4: Construct the corsage by combining net, flowers, and a bow as previously described. Be sure to conceal all individual stems with tape as they are added to the corsage. Finish the design by removing all excess wire on the stem, taping the cut ends, and including a corsage pin with the completed corsage (see Figure 5–20).

FIGURE 5–20   Constructing a Phalaenopsis orchid corsage.

(a) Materials required
for the corsage.

(b) Wire and tape the orchid stem and
place net accessories behind the petals.

(c) Add a bow to complete the corsage.

GARDENIA CORSAGE

The gardenia has been a very popular florists' corsage flower in the past. Its popularity has been recently renewed, and the beginning floral designer will find the demand for these corsages increasing in the future. Gardenia flowers are extremely fragrant, but are also very fragile. The designer must employ special care and treatment in handling and constructing corsages with these flowers.

Gardenia petals will discolor easily with the least amount of abuse. The designer should moisten the hands before the flower is handled, which will lend some protection to the petals. Most gardenias are already mounted on special collarettes when received from a wholesaler. This collarette protects the petals and keeps them in position in the corsage. The construction of a gardenia corsage is similar to that using orchids, with a few exceptions (see Figure 5–21).

Procedure:

Step 1: Remove the gardenia carefully from its protective box. Remove the collarette from the back of the flower (if it is present). Remove the green calyx from the base of the flower but leave the white tube intact.

Step 2: If natural green foliage is to be used as the background, staple the leaves onto the rim of the collarette. Then place the cardboard collarette under the blossoms by turning the flower upside down and pressing the collarette over the central tube.

Step 3: Run two no. 26 gauge wires cross-wise through the stem at the base of the flower and down its length. Bind a light wire (no. 30 gauge) around these parallel wires to secure them. Add additional accessories to the corsage at this stage, if they are desired.

Step 4: Tape the stems by running tape up to the base of the collarette on the flower tube and then back down to the wire ends. A bow is optional on the gardenia corsage. If it is to be included, place the bow beneath the flower in the same manner as with orchid corsages. When two gardenias are to be used together, prepare each flower separately and then secure them together with tape and wire. Do not place the two flowers in a straight line; instead, offset them with the bow placed along the left side of the corsage.

FIGURE 5–21 *Constructing a gardenia corsage. (a) Remove the collarette and staple background leaves to it before replacing it behind the gardenia flower. (b) Complete the gardenia corsage by adding a bow to the wired stem.*

FIGURE 5–22   A completed football chrysanthemum corsage.

THE FOOTBALL MUM CORSAGE

The football mum corsage has become a tradition with high school and college students, especially during the homecoming football festivities and special school dances. The football mum is generally finished with a bow and streamers that match the school colors (see Figure 5–22). A typical football mum corsage is constructed in the following manner:

Step 1: Select a standard incurve chrysanthemum bloom for freedom from blemishes or bruises. Remove the flower from the stem about 1 inch below the calyx. Most florists protect the flower by a process known as *waxing*. A lighted candle is inverted to allow hot wax to flow around the petals from the back of the flower. The cooled wax holds the petals firmly and prevents them from being pulled loose (called *shattering*) when the corsage is handled or when worn. The chrysanthemum may also be protected with wax that is applied from an aerosol can using a product called Mum Mist®.

Step 2: Wire the chrysanthemum by crossing two no. 26 wires by the *insertion* method and adding tape, as explained earlier.

Step 3: Place five leaves from salal (lemon leaf) or camellia leaf foliage on wire stems and tape them. Place these around the mum flower to add background and support to the petals. Then tape these wired stems to secure them to the central stem. Do not twist the wires any more than is necessary. The floral tape will hold the wires securely without adding unnecessary bulk to the stem.

Step 4: The bow is often constructed from two individual bolts of ribbon having the school colors. Form the bow in the same manner as explained earlier, except that twice as many loops will result. The streamers on the bow will also be longer to match the size of the flower. Tying a corsage bow from two strands of ribbon simultaneously may require practice to avoid bulkiness at the center.

Step 5: If desired, add various accessories to the corsage before the bow is attached. Some common accessories used in this corsage design include the school letters or tiny footballs that dangle from the bow. The letters may be formed from a chenille stem and taped to the central stem after fitting it into the center of the flower. The footballs (miniaturized) are held by metallic cord and tied to the center of the bow.

Step 6: Add the bow to the central stem at the base of the flower. Cut the central stem to an appropriate length, tape it, and add a corsage pin.

WRIST CORSAGES

Wrist corsages are very popular with teenage girls for dancing because they are not damaged as easily as those worn on the shoulder. The design of a wrist corsage is the same as one for the shoulder, although most are tapered to a point at each end to conform to the line of the arm. The corsage is worn on the wrist as an accessory, so it must not be too large or it will overpower the dress.

The easiest way to construct a wrist corsage is by arranging two equally sized triangular corsages. These are then joined at the center by hooking their stems to form a double-ended corsage (see Figure 5–23). A bow is added to the center before the corsage is attached to a holder. Most florists use a commercial form having an elastic band for the arm and fitted with metal clips that are used to attach the corsage. The metal clips are folded over the central stem of the corsage to secure it to the elastic wrist band. The designer must be especially careful to keep all cut wires away from the wearer and to cover all construction with floral tape neatly.

FIGURE 5–23   *A wrist corsage. (a) A completed corsage. (b) The corsage with the elastic arm band used for its support.*

A wrist corsage may be arranged from any floral material. However, the larger, more fragile orchid and gardenia blooms are generally not used in corsages to be worn on the wrist.

CORSAGE DESIGNS FOR THE ADVANCED STUDENT

The more advanced student may wish to construct more difficult corsage designs. Several of these advanced corsage styles are presented in this section to demonstrate the various techniques required. A student should have mastered all of the techniques described for the previous corsages before attempting these styles.

Gladiolus Corsage—Glamellia

The gladiolus flower may be used to construct various styles of corsages. The most common use of gladiolus blooms is in a *glamellia* corsage. The glamellia is fashioned from the various sizes of buds and florets from a gladiolus spike to resemble a camellia flower.

The buds and florets must be placed properly to keep the face of the finished flower as flat as possible. The center bud and each added floret should meet at the same height for proper balance. The number of florets required to complete the glamellia corsage will depend on the sizes of the florets used and the desired ultimate size of the finished flower (see Figure 5–24). The following steps are required in the construction of a glamellia corsage:

Step 1: Obtain five to seven graded sizes of fresh gladiolus florets. One of the buds must be tight, without the stamens showing. At least three florets should be fully open. Select five camellia or salal leaves and trim them with scissors to suit the size of the corsage. Wire them to form stems and then tape the wires.

Step 2: Remove the lower portion of the calyx from the larger bud and florets. This is done easily by inserting the thumb inside the florets. Cut the end of the gladiolus floret at an angle just above the thumbnail with a sharp knife. Cut each floret in the same manner. If done correctly, the stamens will fall from the bottom of the flower without causing it to split.

Step 3: Wire the tightest bud by inserting two 6-inch lengths of no. 30 wire at 90-degree angles to each other and taping them to form a stem.

Step 4: Add each successive floret in increasing sizes by fastening them securely with two wires. The wires should pierce the folds of the florets to hold them securely without cutting the petals. Bend the wires downward to form the central stem.

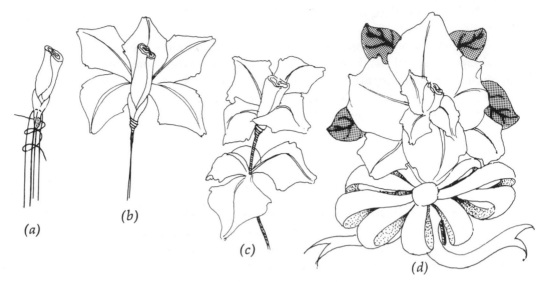

FIGURE 5–24   *The glamellia corsage. (a) Wire a partially opened gladiolus floret and clip off its top. (b) Add additional florets. (c) Continue adding larger florets in a spiral fashion. (d) A completed glamellia corsage.*

Step 5: Add the florets at the proper height to keep the face of the glamellia flattened. Add the florets in a spiral fashion as the flower is constructed. Cut the top ½ to ¾ inch from the center buds to give a more natural appearance to the completed flower.

Step 6: Finish the glamellia corsage by adding the leaves around the back of the flower. Tape the central stem tightly and shape it to form a strong support for the flower. Then place a bow at the base of the flower and the cut stems and tape the wires.

Strelitzia (Bird-of-Paradise) Corsage

The bird-of-paradise flower is unique in shape. The striking floret segments create an exotic allure that is unmatched by other flowers. This corsage can be created with the single flower type only or it can be combined with many others. Since the texture of the strelitzia flower is quite coarse, this corsage design should be used only when either a dramatic effect is desired or for more informal occasions. The strelitzia corsage is created in the following manner:

Step 1: The size of the strelitzia corsage will depend upon the number and size of the individual blooms selected. Most of these corsages are constructed with the florets from two flowers; however, one bloom can be made into an attractive design. Select two well-formed and slightly expanded bloom pods for the corsage.

Step 2: Separate the florets individually from the strelitzia pods (calyx). Either gently tease these out of the calyx slit or divide the pod by slicing it carefully with a knife. Once the florets are removed, discard the pods.

Step 3: Place each of the individual yellow-orange petals and the blue spears on a wired stem. The floret bases may be cut down in size, if necessary, before wiring. Stem the florets with a no. 28 wire using the wrapped wiring method. Tape each stem.

Step 4: Assembling the corsage is similar to the method used for shaping carnations or roses into a crescent-shaped style. Add glamor leaves and net puffs to this design to separate and fill the corsage. When arranging these florets, be careful to prevent crowding. The spears and petals will point in a line that carries the curve of the crescent in this design.

Step 5: Place the florets in position as you would any other flower in the corsage. Use tape after each third or fourth stem to secure them in place. Add the bow to the lower left side of the design. Arrange the florets so that the dark blue spears are located at the focal point. Allow some of the florets to extend downward from the focal area and across the bow. Finish the corsage by taping the cut ends and adding a corsage pin.

Corsages for the Hair

Floral pieces that may be worn in the hair are popular for women at special occasions. Women may have their hair styled to accommodate a special corsage to be worn at a wedding or elegant party (see Figure 5–25). It is important that the flowers remain as close to the hair as possible for this design. The corsage is constructed in a teardrop shape so it will conform to the shape of the head. A bow may be used but is not always necessary. Net glamor leaves replace the foliage used in other corsages. This corsage is attached by using either bobby pins or wiring it to a small hair comb. The corsage flowers will require adjustment once attached to form them into the contours of the coiffure.

FIGURE 5–25
Corsage for the hair

(a) A completed hair corsage.

(b) The corsage is wired to a small comb for attachment to the hair.

FIGURE 5–26   A completed nosegay design (explanation on page 146).

Nosegay Arrangements

The nosegay is designed to be carried rather than worn. The flowers are arranged in a globular shape with the stems forming a handle. The flowers are grouped together so they appear to radiate from a single point. Like the wrist corsage, the nosegay is very popular with teenage girls for special dances. The nosegay design is also the basis for the handheld colonial and cascade wedding bouquets. However, the typical nosegay arrangement is smaller and contains fewer flowers than a wedding bouquet. The steps in constructing the nosegay design are described in more detail in Chapter 8.

Flowers to be used in a nosegay are wired on long stems to facilitate handling and to form a central handle. Many florists prefer to use a net foundation as a center of the nosegay. This is formed by making several loops from net and placing this on a single wire. The individual flowers are then fitted into the folds of the net. The flowers are placed first at the center and gradually spiraled to the outside perimeter.

The nosegay is completed by placing either net fans, foliage (leather-leaf fern), or satin leaves as a background around the outside edges of the design. Commercial nosegay holders are available for supporting the bouquet. When these are to be used, the wired flowers and net may be pulled through the hole in the center of the form. When all of the flowers have been assembled in the nosegay, the holder is secured with pins or wires. The handle is shaped by taping the assemblage of wires together. The handle is then wrapped with satin ribbon, reverse side out, to cover the sticky floral tape. A bow and streamers may then be attached at the top of the nosegay behind the holder (see Figure 5–26 on page 145).

SELECTED REFERENCES

BENZ, M. *Flowers: Geometric Form,* 3rd ed. Houston, Tex.: San Jacinto Publishing Company, 1966.

CHEETWOOD, J. E., and J. R. CONNELL. *Analysis of the Retail Florist Occupation.* The Instructional Materials Laboratory. Columbus: Ohio State University, 1974.

GORDON, R. L. *Professional Flower Arranging for Beginners.* New York: Arco Publishing Company, 1974.

McDANIEL, G. L. *Ornamental Horticulture.* Reston, Va.: Reston Publishing Company, 1979.

Retail Flower Shop Operation and Management. Department of Agricultural Education. University Park, Pa.: Pennsylvania State University, 1968.

STRATMAN, T. S. *Retail Floriculture, Book II: Designing and Care of Flowers and Foliage.* Ohio Agricultural Education Curriculum Materials Service. Columbus: Ohio State University, 1976.

TERMS TO KNOW

Boutonniere	Feathered flowers	Glamellia
Corsage	Hook method	Nosegay
Crosswire method	Insertion method	Waxing

STUDY QUESTIONS

1. Describe how the principles and elements of design are used in corsage construction.
2. List the various methods used for wiring flower stems in corsage construction and explain how each is adapted to specific types of flowers.
3. Explain why the natural stems of flowers are substituted with wires and florist tape for corsage construction.
4. Describe the process of waxing chrysanthemum flowers and explain why this is done.
5. Why would orchids and gardenias not be used in a wrist corsage?
6. Special care must be taken in handling gardenias. Explain why and describe the method used in handling a gardenia when constructing a corsage.
7. List the types of flowers that are suitable for boutonnieres.

SUGGESTED ACTIVITIES

1. Practice wiring and taping flower stems to be used in corsages.
2. Construct different types of net accessories for use in corsages.
3. Practice constructing bows for corsages using inexpensive satin ribbon until the techniques have been learned.
4. Invite a professional floral designer to your class to demonstrate the construction of various corsage styles.
5. Feather a carnation and construct a corsage using the florets.
6. Practice making different styles of corsages using net, leaves, flowers, accessories, and a bow.

CHAPTER 6:

Dried and Everlasting Designs

The art of flower arranging need not be limited to fresh cut flowers. Many flower lovers enjoy having lovely arrangements around their homes and offices every day, but simply cannot afford to purchase them on a routine basis. Most flower purchasers prefer fresh flower arrangements for gifts and for special occasion use at home. For many years the polyethylene plastic imitation flowers have carried the name artificial flowers. The early plastic flower types indeed were merely poor imitations that resembled lifeless shapes and were rarely mistaken for the real items. This concept has changed recently with the general acceptance of higher-quality imitations in everlasting flowers. The popularity of long-lasting arrangements has influenced the commercial florist industry, where a greater portion of the florist design business is directed toward the sale of these everlasting floral pieces.

The fascination for novelty items as substitutes for flowers in arrangements had its beginnings during the late Victorian period when flowers were fashioned from any conceivable source: shells, beads, paper, feathers, and even human hair. These fads have emerged periodically during the twentieth century, each time with a little more artistic design and quality being applied. Of course, there is no substitute for fresh flowers that are alive in an arrangement. But flowers do not remain at their peak for extended periods of time. The introduction of high-quality silk flowers has shown the consumer that very beautiful everlasting arrangements may be enjoyed daily without compromising design and the appreciation for fresh flowers.

Dried flowers and foliages have been used in floral designs since the earliest periods of art history. Today, the modern floral arranger has such a wide array of commercially prepared dried plant materials from which to select that there is no limit to creativity in design. For those individuals who wish to preserve their favorite flowers for creating long-lasting designs, methods are available for doing this.

The creativity of the designer is not hampered by the requirement that a container must hold water when a dried flower or everlasting arrangement is being constructed. Many of the accessories, containers, and flower items themselves may be easily collected by the arranger. Creating these everlasting arrangements differs little from those used for fresh flower designs. The construction techniques for dried and everlasting arrangements and descriptions of their mechanics are discussed in this chapter.

TYPES OF DRIED AND EVERLASTING FLOWERS

Permanent Flowers

The everlasting flowers fashioned from colored polyethylene plastic have evolved from the early copies that were brittle and unworkable to those that are fancy and easily used in decorative arrangements. Modern permanent flowers are truer to the color of the actual flowers, flexible, washable, and generally duplicate flowers in most details. This increase in quality for the finer permanent flowers sometimes makes it difficult to distinguish between the fresh flowers and the permanent copies without a closer inspection.

Permanent flowers have found many practical uses in our lives, where fresh flower arrangements are not feasible. Arrangements may be created for display beside a grave marker in a cemetery, for example. Fresh flower arrangements may not withstand the harsh conditions encountered in this environment. Permanent green plants are also used often in planters where light and care are so lacking that live plants could simply not survive. Permanent flowers are available in virtually every color of the more familiar flower species. These may be used in creating color schemes for homes and public buildings to aid in tying in the decor of the surroundings. Many homes are decorated with key arrangements that can be changed with the seasons to create a different mood. With this wide diversity of plant material, a skilled designer may also create elaborate and colorful window designs for a retail store front. This would not be practical if the designer were limited to the use of fresh cut flowers alone.

The primary advantage to designing permanent flower arrangements is that they may be constructed months in advance of their sale or use. The retail floral designer can construct the many arrangements needed for the Christmas season during the slack periods of summer. The arrangements may be made up for all of the special holidays and seasons without needing to give them special care or handling. If the arrangements accumulate some dust or become soiled, they may be simply rinsed with detergent water. This is also done to restore their luster in the home.

Permanent flowers are available in all ranges of quality, prices per unit, and sizes. The more expensive permanent flowers are generally the larger flowers that are more realistic in color and detail to the true type. Often, several flowers are molded together on a stem to form a spray. These may be simply removed by cutting their wired stems apart with a wire cutter. The individual stems may then be placed on a pick before being inserted in the holder. The entire spray is generally not used as it comes from the manufacturer, except when filler flowers or foliages are used.

Silk Flowers

Silk flowers are the most beautiful and decorative of the everlasting flower types. These are highly fashionable recreations of the artificial flowers that were once used in Victorian flower arrangements. These silk flowers are not at all inexpensive, but offer the designer the ability to create soft and delicate arrangements in the most impressive pastels and true floral colors. Because of the high-quality material and craftsmanship used in their construction, they may be used for nearly any decorating purpose. Silk flowers and foliages are available in a wide array of color tones and flower types. These can be combined by the designer to create nearly any style of flower arrangement that can be constructed with fresh flowers. Florists are now creating beautiful silk flower corsages and even wedding designs so that they might be enjoyed for years instead of days.

Silk flowers are constructed on individually wired stems with foliage so that they may be used without separation. These are often sold either by the dozen in wholesale packages, or at retail by the individual stem.

Dried Flowers and Plant Material

Dried flowers and plants have been used to decorate homes for many centuries. During the earliest years of history, the favored herbs, spices, fruits, and vegetables were dried as a means for preserving them. These were often hung in the kitchen area or placed with their stems in useful containers as adornments until they were needed. During the Georgian and Victorian eras, flowers and foliages were pressed between books to form nearly two-dimensional arrangements. These were hung on walls and later framed as their popularity grew. These early twentieth-century dried flowers were often rather pale and lifeless in appearance because of the drying techniques that were used. Generally, plants were collected from the wild or the garden after they had become dried naturally in the sun. Ornamental grasses, cones, dried berries, and calyx cups were favorite dried materials used during these earlier days of flower arranging.

More modern techniques preserve the colors and the fragile daintiness of flowers used in arrangements. Plant material is gathered from all parts of the world and processed for marketing in the United States (see Table 6–1, page 157). Many dried plants are so sought after that their cultivation and harvest are strictly controlled to prevent their losses from the landscape. The creative designer will learn to select or fashion these materials to suit specific needs. The commercially available dried materials are generally the most exotic or unique, but are also the most expensive to use in designs (see Figure 6–1).

FIGURE 6–1   *An assortment of commercial dried plant material, including eleven of the most popular and attractive.*

(a) yarrow   (b) mini cardone   (c) floral butts

(d) star flowers

(e) protea

(f) oak leaves

(g) eryanthus plumes

FIGURE 7   (Continued)

(i) *spiral cone*

(h) *straw flowers*

(j) *lotus pod*

(k) *wild oats*

Table 6–1: Commercially Available Dried Plant Materials.

Flowers

Campo flowers	Gypsophila	Star flowers
Cattails	Gypsy grass	Straw flowers
Centaurea	Happy flowers	Statice
Everlastings	Hill flowers	Wild yarrow
Floral butts		

Foliages

Areca palm	Italian fern	Sago palm
Bracken fern	Magnolia leaves	Salal (lemon leaf)
Cedar	Maple leaves	Scotch broom
Crinklebush	Oak leaves	Shredded palm
Eucalyptus	Palmetto palm	Stump moss
Huckleberry	Ruscus	

Pods and Cones

Akee pod	Florentine pod	Pubescen cone
Apple-of-Peru pod	Grandiflorum cone	Salignum cone
Begun fruit pod	Green Ebony pod	Sandlewood cone
Bittersweet	Honesty	Spanish thistle
Cardone pod	Lotus pod	Spiral cone
Carob pod	Mesta Bloom pod	Spruce cone
Cedar rose	Mushrooms	Teasel pod
Cotton boll	Pine cone	Wild lily pod
Decorum cone	Plumosum cone	Wood rose
Devil's claws pod	Proteas	

Ornamental Grasses

Ammophila	Lagurus	Sea oats
Barley	Munni grass	Setoria
Bromus	Oat grass	Uva stalks
Broom corn	Oriental grass	Wheat
Eryanthus plumes	Pampas grass	Wild oats
Feather grass	*Poa praetensis*	
Fountain grass	Rainbow grass	

CONSTRUCTING ARRANGEMENTS WITH DRIED AND EVERLASTING MATERIALS

The floral designer will find a wide selection of mechanical devices available for creating arrangements using everlasting plant materials. Since these floral types do not require water, many of the arranging techniques used for cut flower designs may be modified for these materials. Containers that hold water are no longer required, so the florist is free to utilize any item that will enhance the design and conceal the mechanics. Stem supports and stem extensions that are used with these permanent flowers are also often quite different from those described for arranging fresh cut flowers. The major differences in the materials used for constructing the dried and everlasting arrangements are described.

Containers

Dried and everlasting arrangements may be constructed in a wide assortment of containers, including any of those types used for fresh flower designs. Creative designs may be placed in woven baskets for a springtime effect. Miniaturized arrangements may be created in ornate snuff boxes, pill boxes, or oriental cricket boxes. Many modern everlasting designs are not arranged in conventional containers, but are placed on driftwood, plaques, or in clear cubes or domes (see Figure 6–2). The creative designer may find many uses for everlasting flowers where fresh cut flowers are not always suitable.

Holding Devices

Since water is not required in containers that are used with everlasting flowers and material, a greater choice in stem-holding devices is available to the designer. The support materials are selected according to the style of the container, the design to be arranged, and the nature of the stems to be anchored. The most commonly used stem-holding devices for everlasting flowers include styrofoam, floral foam, needlepoints, and cage holders of various styles (see Figure 6–3).

Styrofoam: Dried and everlasting arrangements have been anchored in blocks cut from styrofoam sheets for many years. Florists have found styrofoam to be a versatile aid in arranging everlasting designs because it can be easily shaped and molded to fit a variety of functions. Styrofoam is available in 1-foot by 3-foot sheets in either ½-inch, 1-inch, or 2-inch thicknesses. The designer may fashion the sheets into any desired shape

FIGURE 6–2 *A dried arrangement of yarrow, burned palmetto leaves, wheat,
statice, and lagurus constructed on a banana leaf.*

FIGURE 6–3 *An assortment of holding devices for permanent designs that
includes floral foam, Bar-Fast®, styrofoam, needlepoint holders,
and a cage holder filled with floral clay.*

by cutting it with either a dampened knife or a saw. Styrofoam may be further shaped by sanding it with another scrap piece of styrofoam to smooth rough edges.

The styrofoam may be obtained in various functional colors for use in designs including the popular colors of white, red, green, and brown. White styrofoam may also be colored with floral tint spray paints. A more natural appearance may be created in a design when the styrofoam block is covered with a layer of sphagnum sheet moss (see Figure 6–4). This moss is sold in thin layers that may be broken or shaped to fit the surface to be covered. The moss is secured to the styrofoam with *greening* pins (florists' hairpins).

The styrofoam blocks are first cut to fit the container or to serve as the base of the design. For most applications, the styrofoam must be secured firmly to the base of the container. This may be done by several methods. Woven baskets pose a special problem for securing the styrofoam block. Two wires running from below the block through the bottom of the basket may be tied at the top of the block (see Figure 6–5). This technique will anchor the block securely in the basket.

Several simple methods are available for securing a styrofoam block to a glass, wooden, or pottery container. The block may be secured with hot glue, which is fed from a glue gun. The block is set in place and the hot glue is delivered around the edges to seal it to the base of the container. Hot wax or paraffin may be heated in a shallow pan for use as an adhesive. When the wax is hot, the styrofoam block is dipped into it to coat the base. The block is then quickly pressed into the container and pressure is applied until the wax cools. A special brand of floral clay called Cling® may be used to secure styrofoam to containers also. This product is an extremely sticky, water-proof adhesive that finds many uses in floral designing. It is sold in both white and green colors in 60-foot rolls. To secure styrofoam to any surface, small pieces of Cling® are placed around the edges of the bottom surface of the block. When the block is firmly pressed to the bottom of the container, it will form a suitable bond with the container.

Heavy stems and those placed on heavy wires may be inserted directly into the styrofoam with little effort. Smaller, more fragile stems must be placed on one of the various types of picks. When this is done, the stems will not break or shift their position when inserting them into the block.

Floral Foams: The introduction of floral foam products to the florist industry has greatly simplified the construction of both fresh flower and everlasting arrangements. Foam products are available in several styles and

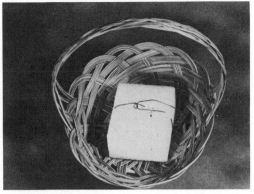

FIGURE 6–4
A styrofoam block is made more natural in appearance for use as a stem anchor by covering it with sheet moss anchored with greening pins.

FIGURE 6–5
Foam stem blocks are secured to woven baskets by wires brought through the base and tied at the top of the block.

colors to aid the designer. The fragile and brittle stems of dried flowers may be easily inserted into these foams without placing them first on picks.

Although the floral foams designed for cut flowers may be used, many foam products have been developed specifically for everlasting arrangements (see Figure 6–6). The standard, general-purpose foams for dry arrangements include the products called Sahara® and Lava® foam, which do not include any adhesives. Woody and heavy stems do not remain secured well in these foams, especially when the arrangement is moved often. For more secure arrangements, an adhesive has been added

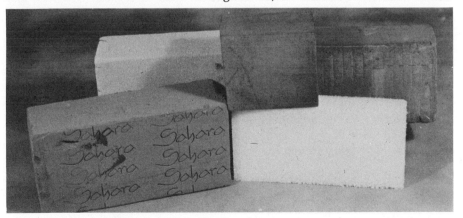

FIGURE 6–6   *Assortment of products used with dried and everlasting flowers. Back row from left: Colour® Foam, Lava® Foam; front row from left: Sahara® Foam, Bar-Fast® Foam, and styrofoam.*

in the product called Bar-Fast® foam. The adhesive dries upon exposure to air after the flower stems have been inserted in the foam block. These standard foam products are available in brown-colored bricks, but more interesting and creative designs may be arranged in Colour-Foam®. This is a floral foam for use with either fresh or everlasting flowers that is available in a wide assortment of colors. The designer may wish to sculpt the foam to create distinctive arrangements.

The floral foams are not as firm as styrofoam, so they cannot be anchored to a container with glue or floral clay. The foam block can be secured with hot wax or paraffin in the same manner as with styrofoam, however. Normally, the foam block is either wedged into the container to secure it, or it must be held in place by some other method. A plastic holder may be secured first to the base of the container with glue, wax, or floral clay. The foam block may then be pressed onto the holder to secure it. If one of the styles of plastic holder is not available, the foam may be held in place with crossed lengths of floral adhesive tape that are secured to the lip of the container.

Needlepoints and Cage Holders: The amateur floral arranger may wish to purchase one of the various styles of needlepoint or cage holder stem supports for constructing dried or everlasting designs. These products are rarely, if ever, used by the retail florist when designing. Needlepoint holders consist of many sharp-pointed nails that are used to secure the stems. The smaller, thin-stemmed flowers will not be secured by these pins because they are not placed close enough for a tight fit. The designer must wedge several stems together or press floral clay into the needles to aid in securing the stems. Cage holders that are designed for dried and everlasting flowers have a mound of floral clay in the center of the cage. The stems are pressed into the clay and are held firmly. The divisions in the cage holder design prevent excessive movement of the stems when the arrangement is moved or handled. The floral clay is rather stiff, so thin stems must be placed on picks before being inserted into the clay. Needlepoints and cage holders are practical stem holders for the amateur who arranges designs often and wishes to reuse the stem holders and containers.

Stem Picks and Tape

The stems of everlasting and dried flowers may require support to allow them to be inserted into styrofoam, floral foam, needlepoints, or cage holders. Several styles of stem picks may be used for this purpose. The most common picks used by florists include the wired wooden picks and the metal picks applied by a picking machine.

Wooden Picks: Both amateurs and commercial florists use various sizes of wooden picks to lengthen and strengthen the stems of dried and everlasting flowers. These are available in the most used lengths ranging from 2 to 6 inches, with a light-gauge wire attached at the top. The pick is applied to the stem by placing it alongside the stem at a point where one-half its length can be wrapped with the wire. The wire is tightly wrapped first around the stem and pick and then around the pick at the base of the stem (see Figure 6–7). The wired surface of the pick is covered with the appropriately colored floral tape (corsage tape) to conceal the mechanics and finish the picking procedure.

FIGURE 6–7 *Wooden floral picks. This technique is generally used for secur-*
ing stems in permanent arrangements, funeral sprays, easel pieces,
and wreaths.

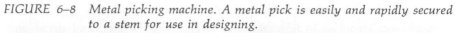

FIGURE 6–8 Metal picking machine. A metal pick is easily and rapidly secured to a stem for use in designing.

Metal Picks: Metal picks are used by commercial floral designers for mass production of dried and everlasting arrangements. The picks are applied rapidly and firmly to the stems by a special picking machine (see Figure 6–8). This is a rather expensive machine, but the time saved in picking stems makes it a valuable investment. This picking machine and the metal picks are also used for fresh cut flower funeral designs that are to be constructed on a styrofoam base.

Metal picks are available in several sizes ranging from 1½ to 4 inches in length. The designer first loads a stack of metal picks in the machine. The handle of the machine is pulled back toward the operator to place a pick in position. The designer then places the flower stem on top of the pick and presses the handle forward or away from the operator to firmly secure the pick to the stem. The serrated edges of the pick are sharp and allow it to be easily inserted into styrofoam blocks. These picks may be used to secure large, heavy stems that normally will not stand easily in a foam block.

Floral Tape: Floral tape used for corsage and wedding bouquet construction may also be used in these designs. The tape is available in a wide assortment of colors that may be matched to the colors of the flowers or stems. Brown tape is used most often for taping the stems of dried flowers, but the creative designer will find many uses for the other tape colors on silk and plastic everlasting flower types. The stems are taped in the same manner as was described for taping corsage flower stems on picks or wires.

METHODS FOR DRYING FLOWERS

The commercial floral designer should be familiar with the best methods used for drying flowers. Many florists sell the chemicals used in the drying process. The floral designers and salespersons at a flower shop are often consulted by their customers concerning these flower-drying methods. The hobby of arranging dried flowers and plant materials by amateurs usually leads to sales of the florist's own products. Occasionally, floral designers may want to dry plant material or flowers to be used in creating their own arrangements.

The creative flower arranger will find that some of the most unusual and attractive plant materials can be obtained without purchasing them from a supplier. Flowers may be grown in the garden specifically for this purpose or they may be collected from the array of wild species available. When done properly, the dried flowers appear as delicate and lifelike as the real living flowers. Some may be preserved so well as to retain nearly all the true colors and fragrance. The art of drying and preserving plant materials is not difficult to master. The process of drying flowers does require some time and expenditure of effort, but the final results may be as rewarding as when working with fresh cut flowers. The arrangements fashioned from the dried flowers and plant parts will last indefinitely when properly preserved and cared for.

Collecting Flowers to Be Dried or Preserved

Flowers should be harvested just as they reach their optimum maturity. Flowers that have reached an overmature stage begin to lose their colors quickly and will deteriorate more rapidly during the drying process. Most flowers should be gathered before they begin to shed their pollen to be certain that they will retain their true petal colors. For variety, do not overlook young buds and some slightly overmature blooms when selecting flowers for drying.

Most seed pods, ornamental grasses, and cattails should be gathered before they open and release their seeds. Seed pods of lotus, milkweed, and a few others may be gathered after their seeds have fallen. The cereal grains, such as oats and wheat, should be preserved to prevent the loss of their seeds. Other ornamental grasses are allowed to open and let their plumes of silk be exposed. Leaves from trees may be handled in two ways. Leaves that form beautiful hues of red, gold, or yellow are removed from trees just as they reach their peak of color in the fall. Some leaves or foliages are collected at any time of the year while still green in color to be preserved by glycerin infusion.

Flowers and foliages are collected during midday, when the flowers are no longer dampened with dew. The flower stems are plunged in lukewarm (110° F) water to condition the flowers overnight in a cool location or florists' refrigerator. This process is as important for the flowers that will be dried as it is for those to be used in fresh arrangements. Adequate numbers of flowers should be gathered to ensure an ample supply and to account for the shrinkage that will occur during the drying process. Before the flowers are prepared for drying, the foliage is removed from the stems. In some instances, leaves may be allowed to remain. However, most flower foliage will not preserve well by the normal drying methods employed. Many types of flowers and foliage may be preserved for use in permanent arrangements by one or more of the following methods: drying by hanging, pressing, burial, or glycerin infusion.

Drying by Hanging

Many flower types dry about as easily by this method as any other. This is the simplest method that can be used, but requires the most time for allowing the flower parts to dry completely. Several flower species may be harvested from the garden in a nearly dried state and the process completed by this method. For other flower types, the hanging method requires about two weeks to accomplish complete drying under proper conditions. Some petal color will be lost and any foliage that remains on the stems may be curled by this treatment.

Drying flowers or certain foliages by the hanging method is very simply done. Individual stems are fastened to a wire or string so that they will hang with their flower heads pointing downward. This promotes straight stems and tighter flower clusters. This may be done by fastening the stems to or draping them from a clothesline or string stretched across a room. The major requirements for preserving flowers and foliage by this method are that the room must be well ventilated, cool, dry, and darkened.

The best color preservation will result in the flower blossoms when the room is cool and dark. Direct sunlight from a window or exposure to too much fluorescent light will cause the colors to fade, particularly the red hues. Cool temperatures are especially important for maintaining the green and red colors in plant material. The best color preservation can be achieved if the flowers are kept in a dry room with good air circulation. A dark basement could be used only if it is not damp. Others choose to use a hot attic, but the drying occurs so fast in this environment that the flowers take on an unnatural appearance. When small quantities of flowers are to be dried, a dark closet can be most satisfactory.

FIGURE 6–9   Dried flowers and grasses arranged in a fireside basket.

Ornamental grasses and cattails are dried by placing their stems in a coffee can or other type of container. The container may be half filled with sand to prevent the long, heavy stems from tipping it over. Most grass heads and cattails should not be allowed to open enough to spill their cottony masses of seeds. To prevent this from occurring and to preserve them properly, a light application of plastic or shellac sealer may be used on them. Cattails may be dipped in a thinned polyurethane satin varnish and allowed to drip dry by hanging upside down overnight. Seed pods and cones to be preserved so that they will not lose their seeds or open their scales may also be treated by dipping them in polyurethane. Cereal grasses can be sprayed with an aerosol application of polyurethane to hold the seeds and culms on the stems.

Ornamental grasses that are prized for their plumes of cottony seed masses, such as pampas grass and fountain grass, may be made less messy by spraying their heads with a liberal application of hair spray. In order to achieve different colors with these ornamental grasses, the plumes may be dipped in powdered Tempra® paint or colored chalk dust, gently shaken to remove the excess pigments, and then sprayed with the hair spray. If an adequate amount of hair spray has been applied, the color will not be transferred to clothing.

Drying by Pressing

The pressing method of preserving is used primarily for leaves that may be flattened during the drying process. Any deciduous broadleaf foliage may be treated in this manner, but the brightly colored leaves collected in autumn are the most popular. Small, dainty flowers may also be pressed to create interesting arrangements that can be displayed in glass-covered frames.

Alternating layers of absorbent paper and leaves may be stacked together. Newspaper will work fine for this purpose. The paper stack is weighted with boards or books to keep the leaves flattened. It is important not to overweight the paper or the leaves will have an unnatural pressed appearance. The pressing process will require about three weeks to accomplish complete drying of the leaves. The process can be speeded up somewhat by replacing the paper occasionally, since the paper is used to absorb the moisture from the leaves or flowers.

Drying by Burial

Nearly all flowers can be effectively dried by one or all of the burial media. Almost any fresh flower can be dried without loss of color or shape when supported during drying by a covering of either fine sand, borax and cornmeal, or silica gel. Each of these drying media will give satisfactory results, but their expense and time required for drying will vary.

Flowers are prepared by first removing their stems about 1/4 inch below the calyx. A no. 16 gauge florist wire is inserted through the stem stub and into the calyx. During the drying process, the calyx tissue shrinks sufficiently to secure the wire. The container should have a top and strong sides. Metal cake cans work better than paper shoe boxes, but strong cardboard boxes are easiest to remove the drying medium without damaging the flowers. This is done by simply punching holes in the base of the box and allowing the medium to run out.

The supporting medium is poured into a rigid container so that the bottom is completely covered. The function of the support medium is to allow even drying along all flower surfaces and to keep the petals from curling. For this reason, it is essential to fill all of the spaces between the petals completely with the drying agent. Single-petaled flowers and those with stiff petals may be easily placed facedown on the support medium. Flowers that have many, closely spaced petals or those with very limber, delicate petals should be placed faceup and the drying material carefully sifted between the petals. The support medium is carefully sifted over and around the flowers to bury them gently as deep as possible. This

FIGURE 6–10
Basket of dried grasses and flowers.

FIGURE 6–11
Permanent arrangement for a child's room.

is done so that the petals are not forced into abnormal shapes. The side of the container should be tapped occasionally while the medium is being added to allow it to settle into all voids and eliminate air spaces.

The flowers are covered with sufficient material to provide enough weight to prevent petal curling. Generally, four inches of cornmeal are required, but only two inches of sand or silica gel are needed over the top of the flowers. The containers are covered with a lid and placed in a cool, dry location. The length of time required to dry the flowers will depend upon the type of flowers, type of drying agent used, and the general conditions of the storage area. Allow about ten days to two weeks for complete drying of the flowers. To test for the completeness of drying, a box may be opened and the support medium carefully brushed away from the flowers with an artist's brush. If the petals are completely dry, the flowers may be carefully uncovered with a brush and spoon. The material is most easily removed from a cardboard box by punching a few holes in the bottom to allow the medium to pour out slowly. The dust and debris that remain between the petals may be removed by directing a thin stream of air over the blossoms. The dried flowers should be carefully stored in shoe boxes or placed upright in containers in a cool location until they are to be used.

The common drying media used for preserving fresh flowers are described and discussed next.

Fine Sand: This is the oldest method used for drying flowers and the results can be quite satisfactory. Only the finest grades of washed, white beach sand should be used for this purpose. These are available from hardware and building suppliers in bags sold for filling sandpiles. The sand should be sifted well before use. If it is damp, it may be dried by placing it in pans and baking at 250° F for 30 minutes. The sand may be reused if it is first screened to remove any accumulated debris and then reheated in an oven.

Sand is the heaviest of the support media recommended for drying flowers. The sand should be very carefully sifted over the petals and tapped into the voids to get an even distribution to all parts of the flowers. Sand is not as absorbent as the other media, so at least two weeks should be allowed for drying the flowers.

Cornmeal-Borax: A mixture of cornmeal and borax will preserve dainty flowers and those having many closely spaced petals. The borax is added to prevent the destruction of the petals from mold during drying. The medium is prepared by mixing one part of laundry-grade borax with six parts of cornmeal. The same procedures as were explained for the sand method are used for drying flowers in the cornmeal-borax method.

Silica Gel: Silica gel is a granular compound that may be purchased for drying flowers. Although it is relatively expensive to purchase initially, it may be reused almost indefinitely. Silica gel is by far the most effective drying agent that may be used for the preservation of flowers because it dries quickly and retains more of the natural petal colors. It is available at better hobby stores, drug stores, and some flower shops as a mixture of silica gel and a color indicator. You may also mix your own silica gel drying compound. Mix five pounds of fine silica gel (28–200 mesh grade) with one-fourth pound of Tell-Tale® crystals (6–16 mesh grade). The blue Tell-Tale® crystals will turn pink when they have absorbed the maximum amount of water from the air and flowers. When the crystals turn pink, the silica gel compound may be sifted to remove flower debris and dried in an oven at 250° F for 30 minutes. The Tell-Tale® crystals will return to their blue color when completely dried.

The flowers are dried with the silica gel compound in the same manner as with sand or cornmeal. Since the silica gel dries more rapidly, only six to twelve days will be required for most flowers. This time may be cut even more by heating the silica gel and flowers in an oven at the lowest temperature setting (about 150° F) for about two hours. A microwave oven may also be used to warm the compound and dry the flowers, if set to operate for only two minutes. Be especially certain that a metal container is not used in a microwave oven. The warm temperature causes more rapid escape of the water vapors from the flower tissues. Rapid drying is important if the natural colors of the flowers are to be maintained. The container used for drying flowers should be kept sealed to prevent moist air from entering. Dried flowers may also be stored in sealed wide-mouthed jars or fruit cake tins with several spoonsful of the silica gel and Tell-Tale® crystals to keep them from drawing moisture. Flowers dried by this technique will be as attractive as any that may be purchased at a considerably greater expense.

Glycerin Infusion: Glycerin is a chemical that will preserve foliage in a pliable, more natural state without causing it to become dry and brittle. The method is used primarily for preserving foliage (such as magnolia and eucalyptus), but may be used for some flowers also.

The stems of fresh foliage should be given a new cut at the base. The bases of woody stems are then crushed with a hammer or split to facilitate the uptake of glycerin. A solution containing one part glycerin and two parts water is poured into a container to a depth of about four inches. Commercial automobile antifreeze may be substituted for this mixture, but glycerin may be obtained from any drug store.

The container of foliage and preservative is placed in a dark location that can be kept cool and dry. The glycerin solution should be replenished often during the preserving process. The foliage is kept in this solution until a noticeable color change is apparent. The foliage will darken to a tan, bronze, or black depending upon the amount of preservative that is absorbed. The green color may be maintained, or other colors produced, by adding vegetable dye to the preservative water. Interesting colors may be produced by experimenting with color dye combinations. The dye will be absorbed into the stem and deposited in the foliage. Complete preservation of the tissue may require up to two weeks in the glycerin solution. When the preservation is completed, the foliage stems are hung upsidedown to dry.

Individual leaves are preserved best by immersing them completely in the glycerin-water mixture. A low, flat pan is filled with the preservative and the leaves placed in it. Any weighted object may be placed over them to hold them below the surface of the preservative. Since this treatment completely preserves the foliage, it may be used in fresh flower arrangements in water without being affected by molds. The preserved foliage is completely pliable and may be easily curved or otherwise shaped to use in arranging. Selected listings of flowers and plant materials that may be easily dried or preserved are shown in Tables 6–2 through 6–4.

Table 6–2: Selected List of Garden or Wild Flowers and Plant Materials Suitable for Preserving and Recommended Method of Preservation.

Botanical Name	Common Name	Hang	Burial	Infusion
		Method & Kind		
Abelmoschus esculentus	Okra	Pod		
Achillea filipendulina	Fernleaf yarrow	Flower		
Althaea rosea (*Alcea rosea*)	Hollyhock		Flower	
Allium neapolitanum	Flowering onion	Flower		
Anaphalis margaritacea	Pearly everlasting	Flower	Flower	
Anemone caroliniana	Carolina windflower		Flower	
Anemone X hybrida	Lily-of-the-field	Pod		
Artemisia stellerana	Dusty miller	Flower		
Asclepias incarnata	Milkweed	Pod		
Baptisia spp.	False indigo	Pod		
Begonia spp.	Begonia	Pod		
Belamcanda chinensis	Blackberry lily	Fruit		
Calananche caerulea	Cupid's dart	Flower		
Calendula officinalis	Pot marigold		Flower	
Callirhoe involucrata	Poppy mallow		Flower	
Callistephus chinensis	Aster		Flower	
Calluna vulgaris	Heather	Flower		
Campanula medium	Canterbury bells		Flower	
Capsicum annuum	Pepper	Fruit		
Ceanothus arboreus	Catalina ceanothus		Flower	
Celosia cristata Childsii	Crested celosia	Flower		Flower
Celosia cristata Plumosa	Feathered celosia	Flower		
Centaurea cyanus	Bachelor button	Flower	Flower	
Centaurea moschata	Sweet sultan	Flower		
Cerastium tomentosum	Snow-in-summer	Foliage		
Chrysanthemum spp.	Daisy, chrysanthemum		Flower	
Cleome hasslerana	Spider flower		Flower	
Coix lacryma-jobi	Job's tears	Seed		
Colchicum autumnale	Autumn crocus		Flower	
Coreopsis tinctoria	Coreopsis	Seed		
Cosmos sulphureus	Cosmos		Flower	
Cucurbita pepo	Gourds, ornamental	Fruit		
Dahlia merchii	Dahlia		Flower	
Dalichos lablab	Hyacinth bean	Pod		
Datura inoxia	Angel trumpet	Pod	Flower	
Daucus carota	Queen Anne's lace		Flower	
Dianthus spp.	Carnations/Pinks		Flower	
Dicentra spp.	Bleeding heart		Flower	
Digitalis purpurea	Foxglove		Flower	

Table 6–2:   *(Continued).*

| Botanical Name | Common Name | Method & Kind | | |
		Hang	Burial	Infusion
Dimorphotheca sinuata	Cape marigold		Flower	
Dipsacus sylvestris	Teasel	Pod		
Echinops ritro	Globe thistle	Flower		
Gaillardia X grandiflora	Blanket flower	Flower		
Gazania ringens	Gazania		Flower	
Gerbera jamesonii	Transvaal daisy		Flower	
Gladiolus X hortulanus	Gladiolus	Plant	Flower	Foliage
Gomphrena globosa	Globe amaranth	Flower		
Gypsophila elegans	Babies' breath	Plant		
Helianthus annuus	Sunflower	Seed	Flower	
Helichrysum bracteatum	Strawflower	Flower		
Helipterum spp.	Everlasting	Flower		
Hemerocallis spp.	Coral bells		Flower	
Heuchera sanguinea	Daylily		Flower	Foliage
Hypericum calycinum	St. John's wort	Flower		
Iberis amara	Rocket candytuft		Flower	
Impatiens balsamina	Balsam		Flower	
Ipomoea purpurea	Morning glory	Pod	Flower	
Iris spp.	Iris	Pod	Flower	Foliage
Kniphofia uvaria	Poker plant		Flower	
Layia platyglossa	Tidy tips		Flower	
Liatris spp.	Blazing star	Calyx		
Lilium spp.	Lily		Flower	
Limonium sinuatum	Statice	Flower		
Lunaria annua	Honesty	Seed		
Lupinus spp.	Lupine	Pod	Flower	
Lysimachia punctata	Loosestrife		Flower	
Mathiola incana	Stock		Flower	
Molucella laevis	Bells-of-Ireland	Flower		Flower
Narcissus spp.	Jonquil, daffodil	Foliage	Flower	
Nicolaia elatior	Torch ginger	Flower		
Nigella spp.	Fennel	Flower		
Oenothera biennis	Evening primrose		Flower	
Ornithogalum umbellatum	Star-of-Bethlehem		Flower	
Paeonia lactiflora	Peony	Flower	Flower	
Papover spp.	Poppy	Pod	Flower	
Passiflora caerulea	Passion flower		Flower	
Physalis alkekengi	Chinese lantern	Pod		
Playtcodon grandiflorus	Balloon-flower		Flower	

Table 6–2: *(Continued).*

Botanical Name	Common Name	Method & Kind: Hang	Burial	Infusion
Proboscidea louisianica	Devil's claws	Pod		
Prosopis pubescens	Mexican screw bean	Pod		
Ranunculus spp.	Buttercup		Flower	
Rudbeckia hirta	Gloriosa daisy		Flower	
Sarracenia spp.	Pitcher plant	Flower		
Scabiosa atropurpurea	Pincushion flower	Seed	Flower	
Solanum mammosum	Nipplefruit	Fruit		
Tagetes erecta	Marigold	Flower	Flower	
Thalictrum spp.	Meadow rue	Flower		
Tulipa spp.	Tulip		Flower	
Viola tricolor	Pansy		Flower	
Zinnia elegans	Zinnia		Flower	

FIGURE 6–12
An asymmetrical arrangement of silk flowers and preserved eucalyptus in a decorative container.

Table 6–3: Selected Grasses Suitable for Drying.

Botanical Name	Common Name
Agrostis nebulosa	Cloud grass
Avena sativa	Oats
Cortaderia selloana	Pampas grass
Cyperus alternifolius	Umbrella sedge (palm)
Dactylis glomerata	Orchard grass
Hordeum vulgare	Barley
Lagurus ovatus	Hare's tail grass
Pennisetum setaceum	Fountain grass
Stipa pennata	Feather grass
Trisetum pennsylvanicum	Oat grass
Triticum spp.	Wheat
Uniola paniculata	Sea oats

FIGURE 6–13 A circular arrangement of silk flowers, dried Gypsophila, and glycerin-infused leatherleaf fern constructed in a woven basket.

Table 6–4:   Selected List of Tree and Shrub Materials Suitable for Preservation.

Botanical Name	Common Name	Kind & Method		
		Hang	Burial	Infusion
Aesculus hippocastanum	Horse chestnut	Burrs		
Albizia julibrissin	Mimosa	Pods		
Alnus glutinosa	Alder	Cones		
Aucuba japonica	Aucuba			Foliage
Buddleia spp.	Butterfly bush		Flower	
Calycanthus floridus	Carolina allspice		Flower	
Camellia japonica	Camellia		Flower	
Cedrus spp.	Cedar			Foliage
Cornus florida	Flowering dogwood		Flower	
Cytisus scoparius	Scotch broom	Foliage		
Deutzia gracilis	Slender deutzia		Flower	
Fraxinus pennsylvanica	Green ash	Seed		
Hibiscus syriacus	Shrub althaea	Pods	Flower	
Hydrangea spp.	Hydrangea	Flower		
Ilex spp.	Holly	Fruit		Foliage
Juniperus spp.	Juniper			Foliage
Kolkwitzia amabilis	Beautybush	Pods		
Koelreuteria paniculata	Golden rain tree	Pods		
Lagerstroemia indica	Crape myrtle	Pods	Flower	
Liquidamber styraciflua	Sweetgum	Pods		
Magnolia spp.	Magnolia	Pods	Flower	Foliage
Mahonia spp.	Oregon grape	Fruit	Flower	Foliage
Nandina domestica	Heavenly bamboo	Fruit		
Pinus spp.	Pine	Cones		
Platanus spp.	Plane tree	Pods		
Pyracantha spp.	Fire thorn	Fruit		
Rhododendron spp.	Rhododendron	Pods	Flower	Foliage
Rhus spp.	Sumac	Seed		
Ricinus communis	Castor bean	Pods		
Rosa spp.	Rose	Hips	Flower	
Salix discolor	Pussy willow	Flower		
Spiraea spp.	Spirea	Flower		
Stewartia ovata	Mountain camellia	Pods		
Syringa spp.	Lilac		Flower	
Thuja spp.	Arborvitae			Foliage
Typha latifolia	Cattail	Stems		
Wisteria spp.	Wisteria	Pods		
Yucca filamentosa	Adam's needle	Pods		Foliage

FIGURE 6–14 *Everlasting flowers simply arranged for use on a coffee table.*

FIGURE 6–15 *This circular design of dried and silk flowers repeats the shape of the container and creates a pleasing accent in a room decor.*

FIGURE 6–16 *A simple design of dried material constructed in a wooden container.*

SELECTED REFERENCES

BENZ, M. *Flowers: Geometric Form,* 3rd ed. Houston, Tex.: San Jacinto Publishing Company, 1966.

BODE, F. *New Structures in Flower Arrangement.* New York: Hearthside Press, 1968.

KLAMKIN, M. *Flower Arrangements that Last.* New York: Macmillan Publishing Co., 1968.

UNDERWOOD, R. M. *The Complete Book of Dried Arrangements.* New York: M. Barrows and Co., 1952.

TERMS TO KNOW

Borax	Floral clay	Metal picks	Styrofoam
Cage holder	Floral foam	Pinholder	Tell-Tale®
Cling®	Glycerin	Silica gel	Wooden picks

STUDY QUESTIONS

1. Explain why dried flower arrangements were popular during early American history.
2. What design period most influenced the use of artificial flowers and how are they used in designs today?
3. Describe the major methods used for drying and preserving flowers and foliage and tell why each is successful.

SUGGESTED ACTIVITIES

1. As a class exercise, set up a demonstration showing how various flowers and foliage types may be dried or preserved.
2. Create arrangements using flowers and foliage that have been collected and dried in class.
3. Invite a retail florist to demonstrate the construction techniques used in creating dried and everlasting flower arrangements.

UNIT III:

Advanced Floral Design

CHAPTER 7:

Holiday and Seasonal Designs

The florist business is largely one of seasonal sales. The major sales periods occur during the sentimental and religious holidays of Christmas, St. Valentine's Day, Easter, Mother's Day, and Memorial Day. Sales during the remaining months are dependent upon designs used for gifts, home and party decoration, and for other sentimental or special occasions such as weddings, funerals, birthdays, anniversaries, births, or illnesses.

The commercial floral designer must be capable of creating arrangements for all of these occasions. These flower arrangements may be as simple as placing a single flower and foliage in a vase or as elaborate as the most elegant wedding bouquets and funeral casket covers. The flower arrangement styles and the plant materials used in their creation will vary according to the theme or purpose of the design and the season of the year. The various holiday and special occasion floral design styles and traditions are discussed in this chapter (see Florist's Calendar on page 183).

HOLIDAY DESIGNS

Christmas

No other holiday period inspires the use of flowers and decorations as does the advent of the Christmas season. This is a season filled with social and family festivities and religious sentiments. This holiday mood is expressed through the lavish use of decorations both inside and outside the home. The floral designer will be preparing for this holiday rush many weeks in advance.

The traditions of Christmas, of course, signify the birth of Christ. This primary theme of the holiday prevails as the designer prepares the decorations for churches and religious events during this season (see Figure 7–1). The nativity scene or *crèche* is used often in plans for religious settings.

FIGURE 7–1   *An arrangement of dried plant material on a plaque with a statue of St. Francis of Assisi who is said to have displayed the first crèche at Christmas.*

Christmas is also a celebration of the winter season. The natural winter colors and available plant material play an important role in home designs at this time. The favored colors of Christmas are white, red, and green. The floral designer will use these color harmonies in most of the arrangement pieces used for decorations. The natural evergreen foliage of pine, spruce, and fir provide the basis for much design work. The red flowers of the poinsettia are traditional at Christmas. The red berries of American holly and the white berries of mistletoe are also incorporated into many designs.

A favorite decoration sold for the Christmas holiday season is the evergreen wreath that may be hung on the front of the house or on a door. These wreaths may be adorned with holly, cones, nuts, or ribbon. The evergreen wreaths may be purchased already assembled from suppliers; however, most retail florists elect to assemble their own in the various sizes and decorated selections. It is not unusual for the commercial floral

Florist's Calendar

Floral Occasion	Flower Use	Date
New Year's Eve	Party/gift	December 31
St. Valentine's Day	Sentimental gift	February 14
St. Patrick's Day	Party	March 17
Easter	Religious/home	Variable dates
Secretaries' Day	Gift/office	Fourth Wednesday of April
Mother's Day	Sentimental gift	Second Sunday of May
Memorial Day	Cemetery decorations	Last Monday of May
Father's Day	Sentimental gift	Third Sunday of June
Flower Day	Home/office	June 21
Independence Day	Party/home	July 4
Grandparent's Day	Sentimental gift	September 7
Flower Week	Home/office	Third week of September
Boss Day	Gift/office	October 16
Sweetest Day	Sentimental gift	Third Saturday of October
Mother-in-Law's Day	Sentimental gift	Fourth Sunday of October
Halloween	Party	October 31
Thanksgiving	Home	Fourth Thursday of November
Christmas	Religious/home/gift	December 25

designer to be called upon to create these wreaths. The wreaths are constructed on circular wire frames. The frames may be purchased or may be constructed from stiff wire stakes that are formed into circles. Christmas wreaths are constructed on the wire frames by tying the greenery with a continuous strand of wire from a spool or paddle wire. This type of wreath is constructed in the following manner (see Figure 7–2):

Step 1: Select a suitably sized circular wire frame or bend a wire stake into a circle. A 6-foot or 8-foot length of no. 9 gauge rose stake will provide a convenient frame. Overlap and bind the ends of the stake together with no. 26–28 gauge wire from a spool.

FIGURE 7–2
(a) Wire wound on a spool or paddle is used for tying wreaths and sprays.

Step 2: Cut boughs of evergreen foliage into sections approximately 8–10 inches in length. Spruce, pine, and fir boughs make attractive foliage for Christmas wreaths. This foliage may be purchased by the case already cut to the correct size from wholesale firms. Approximately one bushel basket of evergreen foliage is required to fill a wreath constructed on a 6-foot wire stake.

Step 3: Place the foliage on top of the wire frame in alternate patterns. Place the first stem at the center of the wire frame and tie it by pulling the spooled wire twice around the stem. Place pieces of the foliage stems slightly below and to each side of the first stem. Then tie these with the wire.

FIGURE 7–2 (continued)

(b) Greenery is tied to the frame with wire.

Step 4: Continue the pattern of foliage placement and tying with wire until the entire circle of the wire frame is filled. Tie the wire firmly as close as possible to the center of each branch to provide a firm support. Do not place the stems too far apart or the wreath will appear thin and ragged.

(c) Holly and cones are added to the greenery.

Step 5: The wreath may be made more attractive by adding pine cones, holly sprigs, or other ornamentation. Place the cones or sprigs first on wires and then incorporate them with the evergreen foliage as the wreath is constructed.

Step 6: Once the circle of foliage has been completed, cut the wire from the spool and secure it to the frame. Then attach a bow to the frame at the point where the foliage was last added.

(d) The finished Christmas wreath.

Evergreen wreaths, swags, and roping are also suitable for decorations in churches and public buildings. Evergreen roping is constructed in a manner similar to the tied wreaths. The foliage boughs are tied onto a continuous length of heavy rope or cording, rather than on wire frames.

Decorations and floral pieces used in homes during Christmas festivities usually adopt the Santa Claus and gift-giving theme. While the colors used are still the same, some basic accessories commonly accompany these designs. Centerpieces that incorporate candles in their various styles and colors are often used (see Figure 7–3). Advent wreaths, with candles that are lighted one at a time during the weeks preceding Christmas, are important florist items. Dining table centerpieces may be diverse. These may consist of candles and flowers or greens; a standard floral centerpiece; or a small red and gold sleigh filled with greenery, holly sprigs, a Santa, and miniature packages (see Figure 7–4). Young children especially enjoy this theme in floral designs during the Christmas holiday season. Some other examples of the Christmas designs that may be constructed are shown in Figure 7–5.

FIGURE 7–3   *Some Christmas table arrangements.*

FIGURE 7–4
*An arrangement featuring
Santa Claus and his sleigh.*

FIGURE 7–5 *Christmas designs.*

(a) *Santa and Christmas tree on a styrofoam base.*

(c) *A candle and carolers.*

(b) *A door swag.*

New Year's Eve

The New Year's holiday culminates nearly a month of festivities filled with parties and gatherings of friends and family members. Most homes will still be decorated in the Christmas theme, so little change from these basic designs will be necessary. The floral designer will most likely be asked to create fresh flower arrangements for New Year's Eve parties and open houses.

The floral designs used for these holiday parties may utilize the winter season theme. Fresh flower centerpieces are designed to be used at tables for dining, the punch bowl, or buffet service. These centerpieces may include accessories that suggest the holiday mood such as noise makers, hats, and horns. These may also be included in smaller arrangements that will serve as party favors.

St. Valentine's Day

St. Valentine's Day is traditionally a sentimental holiday when tokens of love or admiration are exchanged. The floral designer creates arrangements to be used as gifts for this important floral holiday. Men most often ask the designer to create attractive centerpieces or floral bouquets from favorite flowers. The red rose has been the most requested flower for sales at this time. Because the demand and the price of roses have increased, however, other flowers have been accepted as substitutes. The more common flowers now sold include roses and carnations in both the pink and red shades. Other flowers that may be included are red tulips and anthurium.

Floral centerpieces and bouquets may be constructed in decorative containers shaped as a heart or a cupid. Small hearts may also be included within the design to convey the message of love. Other gifts that may be sold for this day include corsages and candy. The corsage may be tied to the box of candy with a strand of bridal ribbon to provide a dual gift. The traditional dozen long-stemmed roses are often asked for by men. These roses may be arranged by the designer in a tall vase to provide a much more attractive floral piece for a nominal price (see Figure 7–6).

St. Patrick's Day

St. Patrick's Day was originally established as a day of celebration by the Irish settlers in America. It is now a recognized holiday by all Americans and is celebrated with parties, green beer, and the "wearing of the green." Party centerpieces feature accessories of Irish pipes, green

FIGURE 7–6   *An arrangement of roses is a popular gift on St. Valentine's Day.*

hats, shamrocks, and green flowers. The all-green bells-of-Ireland flower is a natural selection for these designs. Other flowers may be died green with floral dyes or tinted with floral tint paints. To dye white flowers, they are allowed to wilt slightly and then placed in a bucket of green dye solution at room temperature for several hours. The petals will collect the dye and may be removed from the bucket as soon as the desired coloration is obtained.

Easter

Easter has a variable date each year, ranging from early March to late April. Easter is a religious Christian holiday, but also marks the beginning of the spring season. Spring flowers and flowering branches are desired in designs used for this holiday. Centerpieces and bouquets used for Easter may include the spring flowering bulbs (tulips, daffodils, grape hyacinth, and so on) and flowers in the favored colors of blue, white, pink, and yellow (see Figure 7–7). For the larger designs, Easter lilies and calla lilies may also be included.

The Easter season also carries the tradition of the Easter bunny bearing gifts for young children. Floral arrangements often include this theme in their design. Accessories may be used with the brightly colored flowers to convey this theme, such as colored eggs, chicks, bunnies, and containers resembling an Easter basket (see Figure 7–8).

FIGURE 7–7
A vertical design using
calla lilies and dogwood foliage.

FIGURE 7–8
This Easter basket arrangement
features spring flowers and foliage.

Mother's Day

Mother's Day is celebrated on the second Sunday in May as a tribute to mothers. Sentimental floral arrangements, corsages, and potted plants are normally sold by florists for this occasion. This floral holiday has traditionally been one of the busiest for most retail florists. Corsages are favorite gift items for mothers to wear to church on this day. Corsages are sold in every color, style, and price range, with the Cymbidium orchid corsage being the most popular. By tradition, a red flower or corsage is worn as a symbol of love and honor for a living mother and white flowers are worn as a memorial for a mother who is no longer living.

Floral arrangements for Mother's Day may be styled in a manner similar to those sold for St. Valentine's Day, since this is also a sentimental occasion. The arrangements would not include the hearts and cupid accessories, however. Small centerpiece arrangements, floral bouquets, and boxed cut flowers are generally offered by florists for this weekend period.

Memorial Day

Memorial Day or Decoration Day is a floral holiday in May that is designated for the purpose of recognizing our deceased war veterans and family members. Floral tributes are designed as decorations for cemetery plots. The regulations of the various cemetery administrations in the area will influence the types and styles of floral pieces that may be placed around the graves, so these guidelines must be known ahead of time. Some cemeteries allow the fresh flowers only, which are arranged in brass containers attached to the grave markers. Where the cemetery rules allow placing bouquets or other floral tributes around the headstones, more versatility in design is possible. Fresh cut flower bouquets may be placed in papier-mâché containers and fastened to the ground with stakes to prevent them from tipping over in the wind. Easel pieces in the shape of hearts, crosses, and pillows may be placed near the headstone also. These easel pieces are normally constructed from permanent flowers since the harsh environment would not allow the use of fresh material. These permanent floral designs may be constructed well in advance of the Memorial Day sales period (see Figure 7–9 on page 194).

Father's Day, Grandparents' Day, and Mother-in-Law's Day

These sentimental holidays are set aside to recognize our important family members in the same manner as Mother's Day. When recognizing

FIGURE 7–9   *The wreath is often used as a decoration at Memorial Day.*

the female family members with floral gifts, small centerpiece designs and corsages are most often appropriate. Any of the flowers that are available at these times are suitable. Floral gifts for the male family members might be given a more masculine appearance, however. Most men enjoy caring for growing foliage plants. Small planters may be styled to include a few fresh flowers placed in the container in water picks among the growing plants. These gifts will provide a long-lasting remembrance after the cut flowers are no longer present. Fresh cut flower arrangements may be constructed in masculine containers that suggest the man's favorite recreational activity, such as fishing, golf, bowling, or other similarly designed

FIGURE 7–10   *A Fourth of July design features a patriotic theme in red, white, and blue colors.*

styles. The creative floral designer might also include appropriate accessories in the arrangement that follow this theme (such as golf tees, fishing lures, bobbers, and so on). These floral arrangements are generally not large in size, but should be styled in a tasteful manner.

Independence Day

The celebration of American independence during the July fourth holiday calls for floral designs that are used at parties and for home decoration. This holiday offers a long weekend for the gathering of friends and relatives in midsummer. Arrangements are created with a patriotic theme in containers that characterize the revolutionary period. These might include those shaped in the form of a drum or an old kitchen container. The early American floral style is quite acceptable in the designs. Floral designers may accent the floral arrangements with touches of American flags or firecrackers that are fashioned from colored construction paper. The color scheme for the patriotic design includes red, white, and blue in the flowers, container, and accessories (see Figure 7–10). These colors are difficult to combine tastefully. These arrangements should include accents of the red flowers and accessories, with blue and white used in lesser quantities. This treatment will avoid the appearance of disarray in the floral design.

FIGURE 7–11   *The pumpkin is a suitable container for a halloween design.*

Halloween

The Halloween celebration on the last day of October is a time for parties for adults and the traditional tricks and treating by children. The commercial floral designs sold at this time are used as decorations for parties. The autumn season is well advanced by this holiday, so the floral arrangements should represent the harvest and autumn colors. The pumpkin represents the autumn season and may provide a unique container for a floral centerpiece (see Figure 7–11).

The traditional theme for Halloween is the witch and black cat on a broomstick. These might be shaped from black construction paper to include as accessories in centerpieces. The crescent-shaped arrangement symbolizes the crescent autumn moon of Halloween. This design is most often constructed from orange flowers with black foliage. The black foliage may be obtained by spray painting any suitable material. The crescent design having a witch flying from the center is a typical floral arrangement style for Halloween parties.

Thanksgiving

The harvest theme is symbolic of the Thanksgiving holiday. It is celebrated in most homes with the gathering of relatives for a day of feasting. Homes are often decorated for the occasion with arrangements that

FIGURE 7–12
Thanksgiving arrangements
feature dried plant material.

FIGURE 7–13
The cornucopia represents
a successful harvest.

(a) as a table arrangement

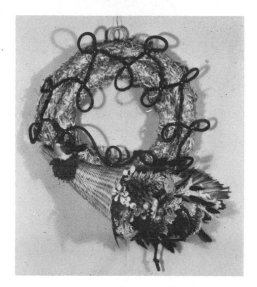

(b) as a wall wreath

feature dried grasses and flowers (see Figure 7–12). The cornucopia or
horn-of-plenty from the Greek period has become a traditional symbol
of the successful harvest and is a favored decoration during this season
(see Figure 7–13). Dried flowers and grasses, fruits, and vegetables are
secured to foam and anchored into the basket in this design.

FIGURE 7–14   Swags may be designed to be hung on both doors and interior walls.

Many dried and permanent flower arrangements are created by florists for home decorations at Thanksgiving. These often include swags that may be hung on doors and interior walls (see Figure 7–14). The picked wreath constructed from fruit and nuts or dried flowers and foliage is very popular for this season (see Figure 7–15). The autumn colors of brown, bronze, orange, yellow, and rust are used when creating these designs.

SPECIAL OCCASION DESIGNS

The commercial floral designer will be asked to create floral arrangements for other sentimental and special occasion purposes during the year. Flowers given at birthdays and anniversaries carry a very special message. Flowers given to secretaries are used to brighten their day. Hospital arrangements wish the recipient a speedy recovery or congratulate them for the birth of a baby. These arrangement styles are an important part of the floral designs created by commercial florists.

FIGURE 7–15 Wreaths constructed from (a) fruit and cones, and (b) flowers and foliage are suitable at Thanksgiving.

Birthdays

Flowers are generally given to a woman or teenage girl as a part of the celebration of her birthday. Women enjoy receiving flowers on their birthday, just as they do at any other time of the year. In many families, it is a tradition to give a teenage girl a long-stemmed rose for each of her years. The floral centerpiece or box of cut flowers that may be arranged at home are the most popular floral gifts for women on their birthdays. Other gifts might include a corsage for her to wear and foliage or flowering potted houseplants.

Anniversaries

Celebrating a wedding anniversary is a solemn and sentimental occasion for many couples. During the early years of marriage, these anniversaries are celebrated with festive partying and floral gifts for the wife. The florist may find that nearly any style of design may be satisfactory. These are generally created according to the tastes and desires of the husband who orders the arrangement.

Anniversaries that mark specific levels, such as the twentieth, twenty-fifth, fortieth, and fiftieth years of marriage, are often shared with family members and friends. Anniversary parties and open houses are often held as a part of these special celebrations. Designs generally consist of floral arrangements for dining tables and coffee tables in the home. Other anniversary parties may be held in restaurants or church recreation rooms. Designs are placed as decoration for the serving table on these occasions. The arrangements may incorporate a number that designates the anniversary year. The container and flowers should also correspond to the twenty-fifth and fiftieth anniversaries. The twenty-fifth anniversary is signified by a silver container and silver twenty-fifth insignia. A gold-colored container with yellow or golden flowers typifies the fiftieth anniversary arrangement.

Hospital Arrangements

Floral arrangements are sent to hospitals by customers to wish patients a speedy recovery. In the case of a new baby in the family, a congratulatory design may be selected (see Figure 7–16). These arrangements are generally constructed in bright and cheerful color schemes to lift the spirits of the recipients.

Many hospital administrations have placed specific restrictions on the sizes and types of floral pieces that may be brought to hospital rooms. Some feel that the soil in potted plants and planters may contribute bacteria and fungus spores to the hospital atmosphere, so these are excluded from the list of suggested floral gifts at many hospitals. It is suggested that the cut flower arrangements should be kept small so that they will not occupy large areas in the hospital rooms. Most hospitals are already crowded with patients and essential equipment and very little space is available for displaying floral arrangements. Generally, these must be confined to a small bedside table or a window sill. A wide array of small and decorative containers is available to the florist trade and may be used satisfactorily for hospital designs. Floral designers should become familiar with the regulations of the hospitals in the area they will be servicing.

Flowers for the Office

Flower days are specifically set aside for providing floral gifts to office employees during the year. These include Secretaries' Day, Flower Week, and Boss Day. Of course, this does not restrict floral decorations for offices at other times. These floral tribute periods are only recently

FIGURE 7–16
The congratulatory arrangement is a favorite for the hospital.

FIGURE 7–17
A floral bud vase is appropriate for a desk because it requires little space.

recognized and have become quite popular with the working segment of the population. Floral gifts for female employees often include small table centerpieces, corsages, or bud vases to be placed on a desk (see Figure 7–17). These desk arrangements must remain small and unobtrusive so as not to occupy a large portion of the space needed for work. Many employers replace the flowers weekly or more often in bud vases for their secretaries in smaller offices. When the employer or boss is a female, the employees generally provide a floral arrangement for her office during Boss Day.

SELECTED REFERENCES

Floral design students will find an assortment of commercial flower arrangement styles that are suitable for specific occasions in the floral selection guides published by the various wire services. Out-of-date copies may be obtained from local florists or newer guides obtained directly from the wire service headquarters. Many trade magazines also publish timely articles and pictures of design styles. Some helpful addresses are listed.

> Florist's Transworld Delivery Association, 29200, Northwestern Highway, P.O. Box 2227, Southfield, Michigan 48037. To obtain an FTD floral selection guide and subscription to *Florist* magazine.

> Florist's Publishing Company, 310 South Michigan Avenue, Chicago, Illinois 60604. To obtain a subscription to *Florists' Review* magazine.

> Teleflora Incorporated, 2400 Compton Boulevard, Redondo Beach, Calif. 90278. For a subscription to *Teleflora Spirit* magazine and floral selection guides.

> *Southern Florist and Nurseryman.* 120 St. Louis Avenue, Fort Worth, Texas 75201. Magazine subscription.

SUGGESTED ACTIVITIES

1. Make a design scrapbook of seasonal and holiday floral arrangements. These pictures may be collected from the various wire service floral selection guides and from home decoration and women's magazines.
2. Create various accessories that may be used with the holiday designs. These may be constructed from colored construction paper or other easily obtained materials.
3. Invite a professional floral designer to your class to demonstrate the construction of various styles of Christmas arrangements.
4. Construct Christmas wreaths using available evergreen foliage, cones, and holly sprigs.
5. Practice the arrangement of the different floral holiday and seasonal designs. Each member of the class may be assigned a different arrangement style.

CHAPTER 8:

Wedding Designs

Wedding designs require specialized floral arranging techniques. Professional designers must have the ability to conduct wedding consultations with the brides-to-be, as well as possess the skills needed for floral design. Any person desiring to become a floral designer must learn the techniques of wedding bouquet and decoration construction. The traditional wedding months in the United States are June and August, but weddings may occur during any week of the year. A florist may have weddings booked months in advance of the actual marriage date. This chapter discusses the construction and uses of some specialty floral pieces created by flower shop designers for wedding ceremonies.

PLANNING WEDDING DETAILS

Weddings have traditionally been a very important part of the florist business. Although the size of most weddings has become smaller in recent years, more people than ever before are being married. Designing wedding bouquets and planning each detail of a wedding with the bride is exciting and rewarding for many floral designers.

The wedding plans are first discussed between the bride, her mother, and the designer at a flower shop. Although the beginning floral designer may eventually be working with the other designers on the wedding, the consultation requires considerable training and experience. The wedding consultant must be able to sell the bride on the best wedding designs while recognizing the bride's desires in a ceremony. The more common wedding flowers used for a church ceremony include floral arrangements for the altar, bridal and attendants' bouquets, and corsages and boutonnieres for the wedding party. Other decorations are generally used to enhance the beauty of the ceremony. These may consist of candelabra and various bouquets for the front of the church sanctuary, an aisle carpet, bows and aisleabra for the pews, and an assortment of floral pieces to be used for the reception. The bride and groom may also desire several table centerpieces and assorted corsages and boutonnieres for the rehearsal dinner that occurs on the evening before the wedding.

The bouquets to be carried by the maid (or matron)-of-honor, bridesmaids, and the bride are the most beautiful floral pieces of any wedding. A high degree of skill and training are required for their proper construction. These floral bouquets may be constructed in many styles and from an array of flowers. The bride's desires dictate the type of wedding bouquets to be used.

The designer must be certain that only the freshest flowers are used when constructing wedding bouquets. Each individual flower or floret added to the design must be wired, taped, and handled carefully to ensure that the finished work will remain as beautiful as possible until the wedding ceremony is completed. The bouquets used in a wedding are very expensive because the flowers are of the highest quality and require tedious labor in their preparation. The final product of this work is a reward to all who are involved in their planning and construction.

The styles of wedding bouquets may vary from a single long-stemmed rose decorated with a bow to those having elaborate arrays of flowers and cascades of blooms. Since each florist establishes the styles to be used most often in the flower shop, only generalized patterns may be taught to the beginning floral designer. Generally, the bridesmaids' bouquets are smaller but similar in design to the bride's bouquet. Each style may be easily constructed once the designer has mastered the technique of wiring the various types of flowers, forming the different shapes of bouquets, and combining the flowers into a securely attached arrangement.

BRIDAL CONSULTATIONS

The bridal consultation interview is conducted by an experienced designer. The consultation generally includes the designer, the bride-to-be, her mother, and sometimes the groom and his parents. The cost of the wedding is largely the responsibility of the bride and her parents, so most of the details are decided upon by her. The major floral plans for the wedding can be completed on this single consultation, but generally several short visits with the bride-to-be are necessary. During the consultation, the designer will use wedding photograph albums and perhaps silk flower demonstration arrangements to aid the bride in her selections for suitable design styles (see Figure 8–1). In addition to the standard professional photograph albums of wedding designs, most established floral shops

FIGURE 8–1 *A bridal consultation is conducted by an experienced designer to discuss the wedding plans and floral decorations with the prospective bride.*

maintain a photograph album of wedding designs that have been styled by their own designers. These albums often include photographs taken at weddings their staff has serviced. Each church and chapel has its own design features that will often influence the amount and types of accessories to be included in the wedding decorations.

The Wedding Order Form

One of the most important items that is used by the designer during the bridal consultation is the wedding order form. This is a preprinted form that lists the major design and accessory categories for weddings. These forms are available from major floral shop suppliers or may be printed by the individual florist. The purpose for this order form is to organize the wedding plans and to assist the floral designers when preparing the designs. The form also may show whether the bride's or the groom's family will be responsible for these separate expenses. The wedding form is filled out in duplicate so that the bride may have a copy for her reference and for her to make notations of changes or additions she may wish to make. This will provide her with a list of itemized expenses and aid her in budgeting for the wedding flowers and decorations. A typical bridal consultation order form is discussed next in the order of subject areas that are normally listed (see Figure 8–2).

McDaniel's House of Flowers
905 East 7th Street   —   Phone 243-5220

Net Price

Bride's Name _____

Address _____ Telephone _____

Groom's Name _____ Date of Wedding _____

Church _____ Time of Wedding _____

Bridal Arrangement:

Attendant Bouquets: List attendants' Names, Color and Style of Gowns, other details

1. Maid or Matron of Honor _____

2. _____

3. _____

4. _____

Head Pieces:

Flower Girl (s):

Ringbearer:

Boutonnieres:

Groom   Grandfather
                           Organist if Male
Best Man   Vocalist if Male
                           Minister
Ushers   Gift Room
                           Punch Bowl
Fathers   Candlelighters
Groomsmen   Hosts

FIGURE 8–2   *First page (reduced 50%) of a typical bridal consultation order form. Samples pages 2 & 3 are on the facing page.*

Church Decorations:

	Net Price
Candelabra	
Aislabra	
Candlelighters	
Kneeling Bench	
Aisle Runner	
Woodwardia Trees	
Aisle Decorations	
Floor Stands Bouquets	
Punch Bowl Decorations	
Cake Decorations: Top	
Base	
Table Decoration	
Guest Book Table Decoration	
Bow for Cake Knife Handle	
Other Decorations:	
Packing Charge	
Delivery Charge	

Charges Billed to:

GROOM'S

Name

Address

Total

Tax

Down payment

Balance

BRIDE'S

Name

Address

Total

Tax

Down payment

Balance

Corsages:

	Color of Dresses	Color and Type of Flower	Net Price
Bride's Mother			
Groom's Mother			
Grandmothers			
Guest Book			
Organist			
Vocalist			
Punch Girls			
Coffee Server			
Punch Server			
Cake Server			
Hostesses			
Flower Attendant			
Others			

General Information: As you can see, page one of Figure 8–2 has space for the names, addresses, and telephone numbers of the bride and groom (page 206). This information should be written on the form first. It will often be necessary for the floral designer to contact either the bride or the groom at times previous to the ceremony to finalize design plans.

Also included in the general information section of the form are spaces for information about the locations and dates of the wedding service, reception, and possibly the wedding rehearsal party. By the time the bride meets with the floral designer for planning wedding decorations, she would have arranged the date and time for the service with her clergyman. The location and time of the day for the service will directly influence the design styles and perhaps the extent of decorations that will be required for the wedding. The designer should be familiar with any existing restrictions or ceremonial rules that must be followed for wedding services and their decorations for the churches or faiths that will be encountered in the community.

The selected time for the wedding service is often the choice of the bride and her family, but is dictated somewhat by religious custom. A Jewish wedding ceremony may not be conducted during the Jewish Sabbath which begins at sundown Friday and extends to sundown Saturday, nor are ceremonies conducted on specific high holy days. Most formal weddings are conducted during evening hours utilizing candlelight to accent the mood of the ceremony. Catholic wedding services are generally conducted in the morning for a Nuptial Mass or at noon for the Solemn Nuptial Mass. This High Mass is conducted for the more elaborate and formal weddings between two members of the Catholic faith. Protestant weddings may be conducted at any time or season. Late afternoon and evening weddings are generally the more formal. Weddings held during the morning and early afternoon hours are traditionally more informal.

Bridal and Attendant Bouquets: The wedding consultation should be held as soon as the dress styles and colors have been selected. This knowledge will help the bride in her selection of flower colors and a bridal bouquet style. In a traditional wedding, the flowers in the bridal bouquet will be primarily white or off-white, with possible color accents in the net or ribbon used in the design. The maid (or matron)-of-honor and the bridal attendants may all carry copies of the bridal bouquet or the bouquets may be quite different in style. When they are to be similar, the designer will want to make slight variations in flower type or color to set them apart from the bridal bouquet. Another addition that might be suggested by the floral designer is to add sprigs of baby's breath to the attendants' hair, rather than having them wear hats. A very attractive accent is created when white baby's breath is added to long black or brunette hair. Floral hair pieces or styled corsages worked into the hair are also very glamorous at weddings (see Chapter 5).

Bridal bouquet and attendants' arrangement styles are determined largely by the preferences of the bride. The florist may show her pictures from the various bridal books or photographs of designs styled at the shop, but generally the bride has very definite ideas concerning the style she may desire. The floral designer may only make suggestions and recommendations, but should always remember that this is the bride's day and her requests should be honored, if possible.

Wedding designs and bouquet styles change often and will vary widely with seasons of the year, geographical areas, and the current trends in design, both in flower preferences and in clothing fashions. Bouquet styles may combine fresh flowers with greenery, dried or silk flowers, or they may contain all dried or silk flowers and foliages. The creative floral designer should make suggestions that will allow the bride to create her own unique arrangement style, if she desires it.

It is customary for the bride to throw her bouquet to a group of young unmarried girls following the wedding ceremony. By tradition, the girl who catches the bridal bouquet is supposed to be the next to be married. Many brides prefer to keep their bridal bouquets, so the florist may design a substitute bouquet, such as a small nosegay arrangement, from a few fresh or even silk flowers to be thrown.

The bride will want to select the style of bouquet, flower types, and colors to be used in the designs for her and the attendants. Whenever possible, fabric swatches of the attendant gowns should be stapled to the wedding form to aid in flower color and accessory selections. The differences between the bouquet styles should also be discussed with the bride and noted on the wedding form. Two basic bouquet styles are customarily designed for the bride and the attendants: the hand-held style and the arm bouquet.

Hand-held Bouquet: The bouquet style that may be held in front of the bride or the attendants is the most popular for weddings. These may be formed in a circular *Colonial* bouquet or styled into attractive *cascades* or other stylized shapes. These bouquets may be rather casual in design, or they may be formal masses of flowers. A simplified method for constructing the Colonial and cascade bouquet styles uses a plastic frame having a small block of floral foam attached. This frame may be submerged in water to wet the foam and the fresh flowers then arranged directly in the holder. The more elaborate the design style, the more workmanship and expense is involved in their preparation. The florist should make this fact known to the bride and her parents during the wedding consultation.

The bridal bouquet may be constructed with the bride's own personal Bible placed at the back for her to carry. The bridal bouquet also may contain a corsage in the center that can be removed. This corsage is then worn by the bride after she changes her clothes to leave the church (called a going-away corsage). The corsage and Bible must be attached to the bridal bouquet in such a manner that they may be easily removed.

The bridesmaids might carry baskets of flowers rather than the hand-held bouquets, especially for a garden wedding. These should be carried directly in front of the waist and held by both hands. The attendants should wear white or matching colored gloves to cover their hands when the baskets are used. The bride and her attendants should be instructed on the proper method for carrying the hand-held bouquets, also. These bouquets are carried in the left hand with the palm forward and their thumb pointed downward. The bouquet should be at the same level as their elbow placed at their side. This method for holding the bouquets will prevent the nervous girls from sticking the bouquet directly out in front of themselves during the service.

Arm Bouquet: The arm bouquet is held along the forearm and across the waist of the bride or her attendants. This style consists of a bouquet of flowers that is tied at the stems with a large bow. This is a very simple design style for weddings, but is not recommended. The bride and her attendants will carry the arm bouquets on their left arms as they are escorted to the front of the church. At the end of the service, the bride and her attendants will be escorted back to the rear of the church by their left arm. This requires that the arm bouquets must be moved from the left to the right arm.

The bride's bouquet and her attendants' designs are not only very lovely, but also help them to hold their hands correctly in front of their bodies. The arm bouquet style and the sometimes used single rose should be discouraged because these must be held either in front or along the arm of the girls. These generally are waved about and allowed to droop in various configurations during the service by nervous attendants.

Flower Girl Basket: The presence of a young flower girl and ring bearer at a wedding will add a special meaning and help to remove the tension from the formality of the ceremony. The actions of the children in the wedding party, no matter what they might do, will add a pleasant smile to the guests. The ring bearer and flower girl will often play a very important part in a larger wedding party.

The younger flower girl may act as grown up as her older sister at the wedding ceremony. The floral designer should anticipate possible accidents, however. A basket having the flowers picked into styrofoam blocks is best for the younger girls to carry, because it will resist swinging or even being turned upside down without creating a catastrophe. When the bride desires to have rose petals strewn down the aisle, these may be hidden in a small area of the basket in back of the picked flowers. However, the role of the flower girl in modern weddings is largely ceremonial, since the strewn blossoms cause the floors and carpeting to become slick and stained.

Supporting Members of the Wedding Party: Corsages are normally ordered for the various support personnel and members of the family. Close female relatives of both the bride and groom (such as the mothers, grandmothers, or aunts) are seated in the front pews or seats nearest the wedding party. They are recognized by the bride and groom with these floral corsages. The wedding form will serve as a reminder to the bride that the other supporting members of the wedding and reception should be recognized and remembered. Corsages are also normally ordered for the women who assist with the registration, serving cake and punch, gifts, the hostess at the reception, the organist, and the vocalist.

The bride may not have the information available concerning the color of dresses each of the women will be wearing to the wedding. The floral designer may find it necessary to prepare corsages with white flowers in this case. When the colors and styles of the dresses are known, the corsage colors may be matched more easily. Wrist corsages may be suggested for those girls who will be serving, because they are more effective than those worn on the shoulder.

Boutonnieres are normally ordered for the male members of the wedding party and close relatives. These include the groom, groomsmen, fathers, ushers, organist or vocalist (if a man), and the clergyman when not wearing a robe. The groom's boutonniere may or may not be more elaborate than the others, but should be different in some way from those worn by other members of the wedding party. The typical bountonniere is constructed with a single carnation or rose, but other variations are possible. The florist should automatically include an extra boutonniere and corsage with wedding flowers to be used in cases where unexpected relatives arrive at the wedding. This courtesy will be appreciated by the bride and groom. Each of the corsages, bouquets, and boutonnieres should be labeled with the name of the person or bridal party member that will be participating in the wedding. Preprinted gummed labels may be applied to a ribbon or stem to avoid problems in distributing the floral pieces before the wedding ceremony begins.

DECORATIONS FOR THE WEDDING CEREMONY

The decorations used in a church wedding service may be as elaborate or as simple as the bride desires. The florist should instruct the bride on the customary and proper floral pieces to be used in that particular church. The floral designer should know the likes and especially the dislikes of the clergy and the church decoration committee. Each church will have specific features of design that must be considered when providing decoration suggestions.

The bridal party is the focal point for any wedding ceremony so all decorations must enhance and focus attention on them (see Figure 8–3). A typical large, formal church wedding service may include some or most of the following decorations and floral pieces: altar bouquets, woodwardia stands, candelabra, kneeling bench, aisle runner, pew decorations, aisleabra, canopy, and window decorations. Weddings conducted in other locations may be decorated with similar ornamentation and floral pieces, but on a smaller scale. The major stands, canopies, candelabra, aisleabra, and carpet runner may be provided by the florist for a rental fee.

Altar Bouquets: The altar arrangements are intended to focus the attention of the audience to the center of the altar and the bridal party. A single large cut flower bouquet arrangement may be placed on the altar table or on the rail directly behind it. A pair of bouquets in tall stands

FIGURE 8–3(a)   *Bride and bridegroom in a formal ceremony.*

may flank the altar bouquet on either side of the altar table and behind the wedding party. These side bouquets will focus attention to the center of the altar.

These main floral bouquets provide dignity and attract attention to the front of the church. The bouquets are generally constructed with white flowers and accented with colors that harmonize with those chosen for the attendants' bouquets. The sizes or numbers of these bouquets should be coordinated with the size of the church, the altar setting, and the number of persons in the wedding party.

Candelabra: A pair of candelabra, generally consisting of seven or more candles, is often placed on each side of the altar for formal wedding ceremonies. Additional pairs of candelabra may be used in decorations for large weddings. *Woodwardia* stands are used in special wedding ceremonies as backdrops for the candelabra. The woodwardia designs consist

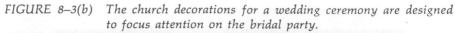

FIGURE 8–3(b)   *The church decorations for a wedding ceremony are designed to focus attention on the bridal party.*

of large palm or fern fronds picked into a styrofoam or floral foam block and supported on a tall stand. These woodwardia trees provide a green backing that allows the candle flames and bouquets to be seen more clearly. In large, formal weddings the candelabra are placed behind the side altar bouquets, with the woodwardia trees placed directly behind the candelabra. This combination of floral pieces and candelabra provides a dramatic accent on either side of the altar.

Aisle Decorations: Pews are normally decorated with large white bows on the ends along the center aisle of the church sanctuary. Rather than having decorations on all pew ends along the center aisle, they are generally placed only on every second or third pew. The bows are taped by their wires to the pew arm at shoulder height with the ribbon streamers flowing along the outside edge. If a floral piece or corsage is to be placed in the bow, it is wired into the center folds of the material.

Aisleabra are especially effective decorations that add formality to an evening wedding. The aisleabra are posts that hold a candle in a glass hurricane style cover. The posts are secured to the pew by a spring clamp. These are also decorated with bows or floral clusters.

An aisle runner is placed on the center aisle of a church for formal wedding ceremonies. The aisle runner is a white carpet that is to be walked upon only by the bridal party members. It may be fixed in place before the wedding ceremony begins and the center aisle roped off at the rear of the church. The guests are then seated from the side aisles. In other situations, the guests may be seated from either the side or the center aisles and the aisle runner pulled into place just before the wedding party is to enter. When this is done, the aisle runner is secured to the floor or carpeting at the front of the altar on a roller. The runner is then rolled down the center aisle by an usher immediately before the bride's mother is escorted down the aisle to her seat.

A kneeling bench is used for some wedding ceremonies for offering prayer by the bride and groom. The kneeling bench is placed in front of the altar over the aisle runner. It may be decorated with bows and flowers in the same manner as is done with the pew ends.

Canopies and Arches: A canopy or arch may be desired at certain wedding ceremonies. A canopy (*Chuppah*) is required at the altar in Jewish ceremonies. At other services, an arch is placed at the rear of the center aisle in a church or at outdoor garden weddings. The Chuppah or other arches are decorated with flowers, foliage, and bows on a special frame. These canopies are either provided by the synagogue or may be rented from the florist. In either case, the canopy is decorated while in place before the wedding ceremony is to begin.

Additional Decorations: Depending on the amount to be spent and the elaborateness of decoration desired, the floral consultant may wish to make further suggestions to the bride for floral pieces at the wedding. Most churches have altar vases that are placed on either side of the Bible or Holy Book. These vases will have a removable liner that may be taken to the flower shop to be filled with a floral arrangement. These liners must be taken to the flower shop in time to prepare the bouquets for the wedding. When the church altar bouquets are used, no other floral designs are necessary at the altar table. For Roman Catholic wedding ceremonies, a Blessed Virgin arrangement might be suggested. A single flower or flower cluster, such as a corsage, is placed below the figure of the Madonna at the side of the altar. A small floral centerpiece or a bud vase containing a single flower with a foliage stem is a desirable accent at the guest registration table.

The windows along the side aisles in a church may be used to display candles and floral decorations. The side lighting with candles creates a solemn mood for evening ceremonies. These candles should be lighted well in advance of the wedding ceremony. As the guests are seated before the wedding, their attention will be focused to the front of the church and the beautiful floral bouquets and decorations.

Reception Decorations

The wedding reception follows the wedding ceremony and is generally attended by close friends and relatives of the bride and groom. A wedding reception is a joyous event where the bride and groom may meet friends and relatives over food and drink. The reception may be simple or elaborate and may include dancing to a live band or orchestra. The tempo of the reception must be detected by the floral consultant when discussing this with the bride. The number, sizes, and styles of the floral designs should be determined during the wedding consultation. The decorations normally discussed for wedding receptions will include those for the cake and cake serving table, the punch table, and the gift-receiving table.

Cake Decorations: The tall, layered bridal cake may be decorated with a floral piece placed on the top (see Figure 8–4). The floral cake top is arranged on a circular metal or plastic tray. The flower stems are inserted into a small block of floral foam. A row of leatherleaf fern is placed around the base of the cake top to conceal the mechanics. The cake top may then be removed easily when the top layer of the cake is to be removed. A cake-top adapter may also be used for this purpose. It is a circular tray with a floral foam block already attached. The base of the cake is decorated by placing leatherleaf fern and small flower buds around it. These are simply laid on the table without securing the stems. The punch bowl and groom's cake may also be decorated with loosely laid leatherleaf fern and flowers around their bases.

Serving and Gift Tables: A round centerpiece may be placed on the serving table between the punch bowl and the coffee urn. The tables may be further decorated with floral garlands or small table candelabra to add to their attractiveness. The centerpiece that was used on the guest registration table may be brought to the gift table for decoration or a separate design may be chosen for this purpose.

Additional Reception Decorations: The cake knife used by the bride and groom is generally decorated with a bow and may also include a small flower bud. At larger wedding receptions, additional table arrangements or even tall, standing bouquets may be desired. The floral consultant must determine the size and expense that the bride and her parents desire for this event.

FIGURE 8–4 *A bridal cake decorated with flowers.*

Follow Up to the Wedding Consultation

The floral consultant will want to discuss the availability of flower types and color preferences with the bride-to-be. She should be aware that those flowers she wishes may not always be available at the time of her wedding and alternatives should be selected just in case this happens. The consultant and the bride should double-check each item on the wedding form to confirm the quantities needed. The consultant may then provide an estimate of costs for flowers, rental on equipment, delivery, and service charges. These may also be broken down in costs for the bride's family and those to be paid by the groom.

Changes in the wedding order may be expected at any time. However, the consultant should contact the bride by the second week before the wedding to confirm the order and the flowers to be purchased. Once the flowers have arrived at the flower shop, it is difficult to make major changes in the order. Most florists require a downpayment to be made on the day of the initial consultation. The remaining balance for the wedding flowers and services is generally expected before the wedding takes place.

The times and places for the rehearsal dinner, wedding service, and reception should be confirmed. Any special directions or instructions should be noted on the wedding form for reference by the delivery personnel. Since the wedding consultant will not always be present when the church decorations are being set up, these instructions must give ample detail to assure that the wedding is serviced according to the desires of the bride.

WEDDING BOUQUET CONSTRUCTION

Hand-Held Bouquets

The flowers, foliages, and accessories used in creating hand-held wedding bouquets are individually wired and taped before being placed together in the designs. The finished bouquet should be very light in weight, so a minimum of stem wires are used. The wired stems are taped together at the base to secure them in the bouquet, rather than wrapping the wires in a tight mass. When the floral designer has determined the approximate number of flowers and accessories to be added to the bouquet, these are individually placed on fine florist wire (nos. 26–30 gauge) in the manner described for wiring corsage flowers (Chapter 5). Foliage stems, such as English ivy and leatherleaf fern, may be wired using the wrapped-wire method, making certain that the wire is secured around at least one of the lower leaves (see Figure 8–5). Net tufts may be added to the bouquet as an

FIGURE 8–5 *The foliage used in bridal bouquets is wired by the wrapped-wire method.*

accessory or a filler. These are also wired and taped in the same manner. White corsage tape is customarily used to wrap and secure the flower stems in bridal bouquets. The tape need only be wrapped over about two-thirds the length of the stem. The techniques used in constructing the various styles of hand-held wedding bouquets are described next.

Colonial Bouquet

The circular shape of the Colonial bouquet is very popular with brides. This style is fashioned after the nosegay designs of the English Georgian and earlier French hand-held floral pieces called the tuzzy-muzzy. The individually wrapped flower stems, foliages, and accessories are combined to form a circular bouquet with a handle at the back. The bouquet may be backed by a lace or plastic doily to provide a form and support for the flowers. The Colonial bouquet may be constructed in the following manner:

Assemble the following materials:

- 1 bolt of white net (6-inch width)
- Assorted florist corsage wire in 6-, 12-, and 18-inch lengths (nos. 20–30 gauge)
- A lace doily (approximately 8 inches in diameter)
- 1 bolt of no. 3 white satin ribbon
- 1 white bow (use no. 3 bridal ribbon), approximately 6 inches in diameter
- 2 boutonniere pins and white corsage tape
- Ribbon scissors and wire scissors
- Baby's breath (Gypsophila)
- Leatherleaf fern
- Fresh, blemish-free flowers for the bouquet. Flowers that are appropriate for this bouquet style include daisy chrysanthemums, pixie carnations, and roses. Other dainty, mass-type flowers may also be used. For this sample design, 18 daisy chrysanthemums have been selected (*see* Figure 8–6 on pages 220 to 223).

Preparations Necessary:

Step 1: Place each of the daisy chrysanthemum flowers on a 12-inch wire (no. 24 gauge), using the hook-wire method. Tape each stem to about two-thirds its length.

Step 2: Remove approximately 10 flower stem clusters from a branch of baby's breath. These may range in length from 4 to 6 inches and the number of flowers in the cluster may also vary. Stem each cluster using the wrapped-wire method on 18-inch lengths of wire (nos. 24–26 gauge). Tape the stems as described earlier.

Step 3: Select 8 to 10 well-formed foliage tips from leatherleaf fern fronds. Wire and tape these in the same manner as described for the baby's breath.

Step 4: Using the white net material, create a series of gathers by folding the net into five individual puffs. Gather the net at the base after cutting it from the bolt and place it on a no. 20 gauge florist wire. Individual puffs may be formed and wired if the designer has difficulty in creating the puffs from a single length of net. Then tape the wire stem(s).

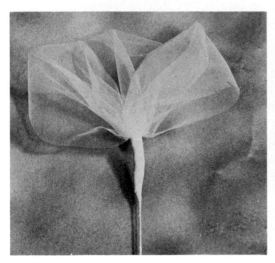 

FIGURE 8–6   Colonial bouquet construction. (a) Construct the net puff first so it serves as the foundation for the bouquet. (b) Arrange the flowers between the folds of the net puff.

Assembling the Bouquet:

Step 1: Place the net puff in one hand while adding the stemmed chrysanthemums and baby's breath between the folds of the material. Allow the flowers to extend slightly above the net. Add the flowers and filler in a random pattern without crowding them together. Continue to place the flowers in the bouquet until the rounded form is established and all of the flowers have been used. The stems may be taped periodically for easier handling during the assembly of the bouquet.

Step 2: Place the stemmed leatherleaf fern fronds around the outside perimeter of the bouquet. Place the foliage from the back of the bouquet to form a background. Distribute the foliage evenly, allowing the fern tips to extend beyond the flowers. Tape these stems to the bouquet to secure them in place.

Step 3: Place the net doily or collar behind the flowers and foliage. Do this by inserting the wired stems through the hole in the center of the doily and pressing it firmly in place behind the fern foliage. If the hole is not large enough to accommodate the mass of wire, use scissors to open it. Then with sharp scissors cut the wired stems to approximately 6 inches long, thus forming the bouquet's handle.

(c) Add a background of foliage around the flowers. (d) Then back the bouquet with a lace doily and wrap the handle with ribbon.

Step 4: Then tightly wrap the wired stems that form the handle with the floral tape. Begin the taping immediately behind the collar and continue it to the tip of the handle and then back to the collar. Be certain that the sharp, cut ends of the wire are adequately covered with tape.

Step 5: Then cover the handle of the Colonial bouquet with white no. 3 satin ribbon. Place the end of the ribbon at the base of the handle with the smooth side against the floral tape. Bring the ribbon over the cut wire ends at the base of the handle and fold it to bring the smooth side to the surface. Press a bountonniere pin into the base of the handle to hold the ribbon in place.

Step 6: Carefully wrap the ribbon over the stem of the handle with each turn of the ribbon overlapping the previous layer. The wrapping with ribbon may be simplified if the wired stem is first curved into its final position to form a handle. Continue wrapping the handle until the ribbon reaches the base of the collar. Cut the ribbon from the bolt and then secure it with a boutonniere pin. Press the pin through the ribbon and into the center of the handle. Be certain that the point of the pin does not protrude through the side of the handle. (*Note:* Before handling the white ribbon, wash your hands to avoid transferring dirt or oil to the fabric.)

Step 7: Attach a white satin bow to the top of the handle, directly behind the collar. This bow is intended to give the bride a pleasant view of her bouquet, while concealing the construction materials. Conceal the wire that secures the bow to the handle with a short piece of ribbon tied with a knot between the bow and the collar.

Step 8: When completed, wrap the bouquet carefully in a plastic bag and place it in a refrigerator. To avoid damage to the flowers, either hang the bouquet upside down by the handle, or slip the handle into a narrow-necked bud vase for support.

The Colonial bouquet may also be constructed more rapidly with the use of a commercial bouquet holder. These holders consist of a plastic handle with an attached styrofoam or floral foam block. The flower stems are first secured with wire and then inserted into the foam on the handle. A metal pick is first applied to the stem bases that are inserted into the styrofoam block holder. These holders make the bouquet construction more rapid for the floral designers. The primary disadvantage for use of these holder styles is that the flowers are not held as securely as with the wired handle method. The flowers may be easily knocked out of position or may fall from the bouquet, especially when the floral foam is used as an anchor.

FIGURE 8–6(e)
A completed
Colonial bouquet

Cascade Bouquet

The cascading bouquet is constructed by first forming each of several floral pieces and then combining them into the final shape. These may be formed into a Hogarthian curve, crescent, teardrop, tapering cascade, or other styles. The cascade style of design is more formal than the Colonial bouquet, so it is often selected as a bridal bouquet for a traditional wedding ceremony (see Figure 8–7). Nearly any combination of flowers and florists' foliages may be used to create the cascading bouquet style. The more common flowers used may include orchids (any type available), roses (sweetheart and hybrid tea), carnations (pixie and standard), chrysanthemums (pom-pon, button, and daisy), irises, tulips, daffodils, stephanotis, tuberoses, and lily-of-the-valley. Of course, the creative floral designer may include many other flower types in these elegant bouquets. An example of the construction methods used for a cascading wedding bouquet is outlined next.

FIGURE 8–7   *A cascade bouquet with roses, stephanotis, ivy, and Cymbidium orchids.*

Assemble the following materials:

- Stephanotis or tuberose blossoms (25)
- Cymbidium orchids (3)
- White sweetheart roses (12)
- Babies' breath sprigs (10)
- English ivy stem tips (up to 12 inches in length)
- No. 3 bridal ribbon (white or other color)
- White net (6-inch width)
- White satin ribbon (No. 3)
- White corsage tape and 2 boutonniere pins
- Assorted florist wire in 6-, 12-, and 18-inch lengths (nos. 20–30 gauge)
- Ribbon scissors and wire scissors

Preparations Necessary:

FIGURE 8–8
Floral cascades are formed by wiring and taping the individual flowers onto a stiff wire for support.

Step 1: Place each of the flowers and sprigs on wired and taped stems, using the proper methods of construction. Place the flowers on 12-inch lengths of no. 26 gauge wire, wrapped with 6-inch lengths of nos. 26–28 gauge wire.

Step 2: Select ivy stems of various lengths, ranging from 12 inches to 6 inches. Approximately three to six longer lengths and an equal number of shorter stems may be used in this design example. Place each stem on a 12-inch no. 26 gauge wire, wrapped with a 6-inch length of nos. 26–28 gauge wire in a manner that will secure the bottom leaf on each stem. Tape the wired stems.

Step 3: Construct the bouquet by forming several cascades from the flowers. These cascades may then be assembled together with additional flowers added to complete the bouquet. Before assembling the separate parts of the bouquet, prepare the following items:

Form cascades by placing flowers on 18-inch lengths of no. 20 gauge wire. Space the flowers evenly along each wire so that they form a continuous row of blooms. The flowers are positioned so they will face in a left, right, or center direction as the flowers are secured to the support wire. Secure the wired flower stems to the support wire with tightly stretched corsage tape, without twisting the wire (see Figure 8–8). Some suggested wired floral cascades are:

- A length of wire with five stephanotis and two roses. Space each flower at approximately 2-inch distances at the floral bases, starting with the first flower placed directly on the end of the support wire. Secure each flower with tape as it is added along the cascade.
- Form a cascade using three stephanotis and one rose flower.
- Form a cascade using six stephanotis alone.
- Form a cascade using only three stephanotis blossoms.

Assembling the Bouquet:

Step 1: Assemble the three orchids into a loose cluster using stephanotis flowers, babies' breath sprigs, a bow, and net butterfly accents. Form this grouping of flowers on a long wire stem to create the foundation for the bouquet and the handle.

Step 2: Create a net puff from the white net. Wrap the net into four to six folds that are each approximately 4 inches in length. Place a no. 26 gauge wire in the center of the net and tape the wired stem.

Step 3: Position the net puff directly under the assembled orchids to create a delicate background for these accent flowers.

Step 4: Place the longer cascade stems and ivy strands below the orchids. Arrange the stems so that they will create a tapered shape to the bouquet. Bring all of the wired stems back along the handle of the bouquet.

Step 5: Distribute the remaining individually stemmed flowers and ivy foliage stems randomly above the orchids and throughout the bouquet to complete the design.

Step 6: Cut the wires evenly approximately 6 to 8 inches below the back of the bouquet. Form a handle by taping and wrapping with satin ribbon as described for the Colonial bouquet style. Attach a grouping of ribbon streamers to the handle to create an accent before adding the bow. If desired, add a series of love knots to the ends of the streamers for wishing luck to the bride. Vary the lengths of the streamers to add interest to the design.

Cascade Bouquet with Removable Corsage

When the bride-to-be desires to have her going-away corsage made a part of the bridal bouquet, the floral designer will have to make some minor changes in the design during its construction. Normally, the cascade bouquet is constructed in the customary manner, but the focal area is not completed. When the cascades and the flowers are placed around the net puff in the center of the design, space is left open for the corsage. An 8- to 10-inch length of bridal ribbon may be placed on an 18-inch length of

FIGURE 8–9   *The bridal bouquet may be constructed so that a corsage in the center can be removed.*

no. 26 gauge wire. This wire is pulled down into the bouquet handle, exposing only the ribbon in the center of the design. A corsage is assembled in the customary fashion and then placed into the bouquet center, with the bow above the flower at the top of the bouquet. The corsage is then securely fastened into the bouquet by tying it to the ribbon streamers that were added in the center. When the bride is to wear the corsage, the bow created when being tied in the bouquet may be loosened and the corsage lifted out of the bouquet (see Figure 8–9).

Arm Bouquet Style

The arm bouquet design consists of long-stemmed flowers, filler, and foliage that are tied together with a large bow. Nearly any combination of flowers or only a single flower type may be used in this design (see Figure 8–10). The floral designer should accentuate the stems by cutting most of them short, just below the point where the bow is to be tied. Only a few of the stems will remain below the bow. All foliage should be removed from the stems and any roses should be cleaned of all thorns. The arm bouquet style is not used often for weddings, but is quite popular as a presentation bouquet for debutante balls and other situations where flowers are provided for an honored guest.

FIGURE 8–10   *An arm bouquet can be used for a wedding design or for a presentation bouquet.*

SELECTED REFERENCES

BENZ, M. *Flowers: Geometric Form,* 3rd ed. Houston, Tex.: San Jacinto Publishing Company, 1966.

McDANIEL, G. L. *Ornamental Horticulture.* Reston, Va.: Reston Publishing Company, 1979.

Something Old, Something New. Lansing, Mich.: The John Henry Company, 1978.

STRATMAN, T. S. *Retail Floriculture, Book II: Designing and Care of Flowers and Foliage.* Ohio Agricultural Education Curriculum Materials Service. Columbus: Ohio State University, 1976.

TOLLE, L. J. *Floral Art for Religious Events.* New York: Hearthside Press, 1969.

Vogue in Wedding Flowers (Current). Chicago: Florists' Publishing Company.

TERMS TO KNOW

Aisleabra	Bridesmaid	Cascade bouquet	Flower girl
Altar	Cake adapter	Colonial bouquet	Maid-of-honor
Arm bouquet	Canopy	Consultation	Woodwardia

STUDY QUESTIONS

1. List the basic flower arrangements and bouquets that would be used for a typical church wedding and reception.
2. Describe how the floral designs used in a garden wedding might be different from those at a church ceremony.
3. Discuss the differences in design found in the hand-held and arm bouquets. Name an advantage for using each bouquet style.
4. Explain why the florist must be familiar with each church and the clergymen located in the community where weddings will be serviced.

SUGGESTED ACTIVITIES

1. Conduct a mock wedding, complete with floral bouquets, accessories, and wedding attire. The ceremony may be held in conjunction with a bridal shop, using students as members of the wedding party. The wedding bouquets may be arranged as a class project and all decorating done by the students.

2. Hold a bridal consultation as a part of a class exercise. The consultation may be directed by the instructor, using students in the roles of the floral designer and the bride-to-be. Make the bridal consultation realistic, using bridal books, order forms, and actual wedding situations as a guide.

3. Construct a Colonial bouquet using appropriate mass and filler flowers. This may be done as a collective effort of more than one student.

4. Construct a cascade bouquet using available flowers and accessory materials. Wiring the flowers and assembling the bouquet may be done by several students as a group project. Some bouquets may be constructed with the going-away corsage placed in the center of the design.

5. Construct an arm bouquet using available flowers and accessory materials.

6. Have a commercial florist visit the class or take a field trip to a retail flower shop. Have the florist demonstrate bridal bouquet construction methods and discuss the various aspects of bridal consultations.

CHAPTER 9:

Funeral Designs

The retail florist sees customers on occasions of joy, love, and sorrow. The circumstances surrounding the death of a loved one bring customers to the flower shop for the purpose of bestowing a floral tribute to the deceased. Flowers portray the traditional emotions of love, faith, and sympathy to the family. Funeral flowers are arranged for the living members of the family and friends that attend the funeral service. These arrangements may be simple or they may be quite lavish. The floral designer uses the same degree of talent and creativity when arranging funeral pieces as with all other specialty designs. Funeral business is not easily predicted, with sales of funeral pieces occurring at all times of the year and with little advanced notice. The demand for flowers at funerals is waning in some areas of the country but remains steady in others.

FUNERAL CONSULTATIONS

For many years, retail florists depended upon the funeral flower business to provide a livelihood. Modern florists must depend on their reputation for creativity and professionalism in design to maintain their share of the funeral business. Florists must keep informed of any deaths that occur and know where the funeral services are to be held in the community. This information may be obtained from local newspaper and radio news and from personal contact with the local funeral directors. This information is needed so that the florists may service the funeral orders correctly.

Soon after the death of a family member, the closest members of a family will meet with the florist to plan the major floral arrangements to be displayed at the funeral. The florist who conducts this consultation with the family members must be well informed about the types of funeral pieces that are sold at the shop, the funeral traditions and restrictions in the community, the religious requirements of various faiths, and the flower types and quantities available for servicing the funeral orders.

The florist who conducts the funeral flower consultation should be aware that the emotions of the family members will be strained under the conditions of preparing the details for a funeral. Unless the deceased person left explicit details for their own funeral and the floral tribute styles to be displayed, the family may not have specific ideas in mind. The florist should exercise careful selling techniques when consulting with the family members. If the florist is not familiar with the family situation and feels that additional floral pieces may be desired, he or she should feel free to ask the family about them. The family will generally need some professional suggestions concerning the floral tributes to be given by other family members, such as from brothers, sisters, grandchildren, or children of the deceased.

The florist makes suggestions based on the current supply of flowers in the shop at the time or from those flowers that may be easily obtained. Since funeral services are generally held within three days of the death, the florist must make certain that an adequate supply of flowers will be available to service the orders for the funeral pieces. This may present a special problem for florists who are not located near a wholesale florist firm or greenhouse. The florist, however, must also be flexible in suggestions and attempt to meet the wishes and requirements of the family members. Although the florist may need to direct their decisions, the floral pieces are an important feature in the funeral service and will become a part of the memory for those family members.

Floral Selections for Funeral Services

The purpose of the funeral consultation is to assist the family members in their decisions concerning the styles and types of flowers to be used in the basic floral tributes for the funeral. The sizes of the sprays or bouquets to be purchased will be determined by the types of flowers selected and the amount of money to be spent on the designs. The florist must be able to direct the family in their decisions for these designs. The basic floral pieces displayed at a funeral include the casket spray, standing sprays, and easel pieces, as well as various bouquets, flowering plants, and flat sprays.

Casket Sprays: The floral piece that is placed on the lid of the casket couch is called the *casket cover.* This floral spray is generally the most elaborate and beautiful of the floral designs shown at a funeral service. The casket cover is purchased by the immediate family members of the deceased.

Casket covers may be of several design styles, depending on the type of service to be held. Casket couches are designed with the lid opening on the left side when displayed at a funeral service. At an open-casket service, the casket cover is placed at the foot of the casket. A *half-couch* cover is used in this situation, with the flowers cascading down the front of the casket. The half-casket cover may also be used with an infant's casket.

A *full-couch* cover is designed for use at a closed-casket service. The floral spray may then be placed at the center of the casket lid and allowed to drape over the front of the casket. Casket covers are not always displayed at funerals, however. Funerals held in Catholic churches (Requiem Mass) and at Orthodox Jewish synagogues do not generally display flowers on the casket. A flag is generally draped over the casket at a military funeral service. The florist must become familiar with the various religious traditions in the community before servicing funerals in the area.

The florist should also determine the styles and sizes of the caskets to be used in funerals, so that the casket covers will be appropriately designed. This information may be obtained from the local funeral directors. The sizes of the funeral hearses used by the various funeral chapels should also be obtained so that the casket covers may fit through the opening when the casket is transported to the cemetery.

Standing Sprays: Sprays placed on easels are used as floral tributes from close friends and other relatives of the deceased person. These sprays are placed near the head or foot of the casket during the service. Standing sprays are most often designed as double-end sprays and are generally large and elaborate floral pieces (see Figure 9-1). These sprays may also be substituted for the casket covers in services where the casket may not be covered with flowers.

Other Floral Designs: The florist may expect to receive orders for various other types of floral designs to be displayed at a funeral service. These orders may be received from relatives, close and casual friends, and business associates of the family of the deceased person. Many of these flower orders will be received by telephone from other cities. The florist should be able to give the caller a verbal picture of each design that he or she intends to create for the purchaser. Often the florist will collect a number of orders together on a floral tribute list and combine them into a single floral design. In this way, each person may make a contribution to the flowers without having to purchase an entire arrangement.

Modern retail florists must provide the best service and most attractive floral arrangements for funeral services, if they are to continue to share in the funeral market. The floral designs should be constructed with

FIGURE 9–1
*A standing double-end spray
on an easel.*

only fresh flowers that will provide enjoyment to the family for as long as is possible. Most of the funeral designs are constructed in a floral foam or in water-filled containers to extend their useful lives. Only those sprays or wreaths that will be transported with the casket to the cemetery may be constructed by picking the flowers directly into moss or styrofoam bases. The fresh bouquets and potted plants are normally taken to the family home.

BASIC FUNERAL DESIGN

Funeral services and the floral pieces displayed vary according to the tastes and desires of the family. A typical funeral might include displays featuring cut flower arrangements in baskets, a casket piece, sprays, potted plants, and wreaths or fraternal easel pieces. The cut flower baskets are constructed as described in Chapter 4, in either a radiating or triangular design. Easel pieces are constructed by picking fresh flower stems into a moss, styrofoam, or floral foam block of the appropriate design. These are supported on specially designed tripod wire frames for display at the funeral service.

The beginning floral designer must learn the basic steps required for constructing casket sprays, flat sprays, and easel pieces for funerals. The flowers selected for use in funeral designs are those that are at the peak of their beauty. Roses, for example, appear best when half-opened or fully opened. Flowers that are in tight bud will not show to their full advantage. Each flower to be used in constructing funeral sprays is placed on a supporting wire (nos. 18–22 gauge). If these flowers are to be placed in a moss or styrofoam block, either a wooden or steel pick is attached to the end of each stem. Steel picks are rapidly placed on the ends of flower stems with the aid of a picking machine. The quantity of flowers used in each of the funeral piece designs will be determined by their price.

A Basic Casket Spray

The casket spray is used to cover the lid of the casket and is often the most elaborate floral piece at a funeral service. The florist takes pride in the design and creation of each casket spray. The flowers may be arranged in floral foam blocks to keep the flowers fresh for an extended period or picked into styrofoam blocks. The support block (either floral foam or styrofoam) is attached to a specially designed casket *saddle* made for this purpose (see Figure 9–2). All flowers to be used in the casket spray are wired to support the stems and blooms.

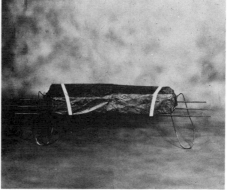

FIGURE 9–2   Casket saddles. (a) Designed for use with floral foam blocks in water. (b) A wire frame saddle for use with styrofoam blocks or floral foam wrapped in florists' foil.

The size of the casket spray is determined by its price, which affects the number and kinds of flowers used and the type of accessories that will be added. Several casket cover design styles may be found in use at funerals. These include the *full-couch, half-couch,* and *lid-cover* styles. Full-couch covers are used for closed-casket services, where the casket spray will extend across the entire lid. These are normally formed to create a cascading effect at the front of the casket and are approximately 4 to 5 feet in length. The half-couch style is used more commonly for services where the spray is placed at the foot of an open casket. The size of this spray will vary according to that of the casket, but is normally 3 feet in length for an adult-sized casket. A lid cover is designed to cascade over the front of an opened casket lid. It is used primarily as a cover for infant caskets, where the entire casket lid remains open during the service. The length of this design corresponds with the length of the casket, generally being 3 to 4 feet in length.

Support Blocks: Two types of support blocks may be used in constructing casket sprays: styrofoam and floral foam. Floral foam blocks are preferred by florists when the casket spray is to be at the funeral chapel for more than a half day. These floral foams cannot withstand extended movement when being transported as a spray, so more care must be taken in their handling. Floral foam blocks are generally first thoroughly soaked in preservative-water until completely saturated. The block is then wrapped tightly in a single sheet of green florist foil. The foil is secured to the block to prevent the loss of water by binding it with string or green florist cord. The foam block is then placed in a saddle frame that is designed to prevent water leaking onto the casket. The block is wired onto the saddle frame using 18-inch lengths of nos. 20 or 22 gauge wire that has been wrapped in green floral tape to prevent it from cutting into the foam block. Floral cord or string may also be used for this purpose. An alternate method for using floral foams is to place them in the watertight saddle frames and secure them with waterproof adhesive tape without first wrapping the block in foil.

Styrofoam blocks provide a more secure support for casket sprays and easel pieces than do the floral foam products. The major disadvantage for using styrofoam is that the flower stems have no access to water. Flower stems may be placed on either wooden or steel picks and inserted directly into the styrofoam block for funeral designs that will not be on display for extended periods of time. Generally, a picking machine and steel picks are used for rapid construction of these designs. The blocks are cut from green or white florist styrofoam to fit the wire saddle, then secured to it with 18-inch lengths of no. 20 or 22 gauge wire.

Water Picks: Florists sometimes wish to combine the security of styrofoam blocks with flowers placed in water for use in funeral pieces. This can be accomplished by using water picks. These are plastic tubes that are pointed on one end to allow them to be anchored securely in the support block (see Figure 9–3). The tubes are filled with a preservative-water solution and capped with a rubber cover having a hole in the center. The flower stem is given a slanted cut at the base and inserted through the hole of the water pick to the bottom of the tube. The stem and water pick are then pressed into the styrofoam block to a distance of 2 inches or until the pick is securely anchored. Water picks may also be required regardless of the type of anchoring block used when the natural stem of a flower must be lengthened (as with orchids) to conform to the size of the design. These short-stemmed flowers are inserted into water picks and then wired onto wooden picks or sections of bamboo stakes.

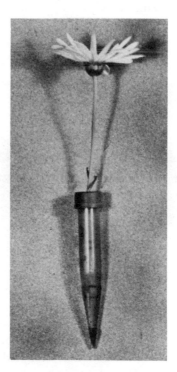

FIGURE 9–3
Water picks are used by designers when fresh flowers are picked into styrofoam support blocks or when short-stemmed flowers must be given a longer stem in a spray or bouquet.

Stem Picks: Whenever flowers or foliages are to be secured onto a styrofoam foundation, some type of pick must be applied to the stems. Various styles of wooden and metal picks may be used for this purpose. Wooden picks with a thin florist wire attached to one end are available in lengths ranging from 2 to 12 inches. Stems are attached to the pick by placing them along the side to a point near the center of the pick. The wire is wound around both the stem and pick and then firmly secured to create a union that will not separate. Modern picking machines have been developed to apply metal picks rapidly to stems. These picks are available in a wide range of sizes. The flower stem is simply placed over the metal pick in the machine and a lever pressed to form a secure bond with the stem (see Figure 9–4). Several small flower stems may be combined before the metal pick is applied. In some instances, the standard wooden or metal picks are either too large or inconvenient for application in a design. Soft, succulent stems may be rapidly picked by simply inserting a round tooth-pick into the center of the stem, leaving one-third to one-half of the pick exposed. The fleshy stem base is then bound by wrapping with a light-gauge florist wire to prevent it from splitting upon insertion in the styrofoam block.

FIGURE 9–4   *The picking machine. (a) The stem is placed over the pick in the machine, the lever is pushed to attach the pick, and (b) the metal pick is firmly secured to the stem.*

Constructing a Casket Spray: A simplified casket spray may be constructed by following these steps (see Figure 9–5):

Step 1: Attach the support block to be used to an appropriate casket saddle frame designed for the size of spray desired. Place floral foams in watertight frames and secure them with waterproof adhesive tape. Wire styrofoam blocks to the frame.

Step 2: Place stems of flat fern, palm leaf, or jade leaf greenery around the outer perimeter of the saddle container. These stems of greenery provide a background for the design and conceal the saddle and support block. The foliage stems are longest along the horizontal axis of the arrangement and create either an oval or a cascading design.

Step 3: Create a pillow effect across the top center of the spray by inserting loops formed from the foliage stems, which have been curved. Fold the leaves gently without breaking their stems and then secure them to the supporting block.

Step 4: Next, add the wired flowers to the spray. First position flowers all around the lower perimeter above the background of foliage. Place the next level of flowers above the first, with the blooms on slightly shorter stems. Continue adding flowers until the spray is uniformly covered. If a draped or cascading effect is to be created at the front of the spray, the background foliage and layers of flowers should conform to this line also. If desired, place a supporting box under the casket saddle to elevate the spray while creating the cascading lines.

Step 5: Place additional greenery or filler foliage between the flowers if required to fill in the design. Add filler flowers, such as baby's breath or pompon chrysanthemums, to accent the design.

Step 6: Construct a satin bow from nos. 40 or 120 ribbon. Add streamers so that their length is equal to that of the spray. Attach the bow to a wooden pick approximately 4 inches in length. The pick is easily inserted into the support block to secure the bow in the spray. Larger full-couch sprays may require larger bows than are used in smaller sprays. Individual bow loops may be placed on their own wooden picks and placed strategically within the body of the casket spray to create a fuller appearance.

Step 7: Once the bow and streamers are neatly positioned, carefully inspect the spray for faults. Add greenery wherever a void or space appears. Check the flowers to make certain that the stems are tightly secured.

Step 8: It is customary to have a name added to the ribbon streamer on a casket spray and other funeral pieces given by the family members. These normally bear the relationship of the deceased to the giver: for example, Grandfather, Father, or Mother. These words are available on adhesive-backed patterns that may be simply pressed onto the ribbon streamer before it is picked into the spray.

Step 9: Before taking the casket spray to the storage refrigerator, add additional water to the container on those sprays in floral foam blocks. Cover sprays constructed in styrofoam blocks in a layer of polyethylene plastic film to conserve moisture while in storage. Drain all water from a foam saddle container before delivering the casket spray to the funeral home to prevent spills onto the casket couch.

FIGURE 9–5 *Casket spray construction. (a) Place the foliage background around the perimeter of the saddle. (b) Create a pillow with the fern in the center of the spray. (c) Establish the size of the spray with the flowers placed at the ends. (d) Complete the base of the spray by placing the flowers along the sides. (e) Add the flowers to create a tiered effect across the top of the spray. (f) Add the flowers until the spray is filled in.*

(a)

(b)

(c)

(d)

(e)

(f)

FIGURE 9–5(g) *Add a bow and streamers to the center of the spray.*
(h) *Complete the spray by adding filler material.*

(g)   (h)

Flat Sprays and Standing Double-End Sprays:

Flat sprays are designed to be displayed on a special frame that holds up to one dozen sprays along the side or ends of a casket. These sprays are generally given by friends and more distant relatives of the deceased. Since they are smaller in size, their construction methods are generally much simpler than with the easel and casket pieces.

Double-end sprays are larger in size than flat sprays and are designed to be displayed singly on a tripod easel. These are generally constructed on either styrofoam or floral foam support blocks in the same manner as was described for the various types of casket sprays, but they do not require a casket saddle frame and are smaller in size.

Flat sprays may also be constructed by picking the flowers and foliages into a floral foam or a styrofoam support block; but the tied spray is more rapid and inexpensive to create. Generally, these sprays are formed in a single-end design without such a base by simply wiring the stems together in a continuous line to form a spray of flowers and foliage (see Figure 9–6). The flat spray may be constructed in the following manner:

Step 1: Select nine standard carnations. Place each on a support wire using the insertion method.

Step 2: Lay three pieces of flat fern in the shape of a fan. Wire these stems with the aid of malin (called paddle-wire or spool wire, nos. 24 or 26 gauge) wound onto a stick or spool. Circle the wire around the stems twice and pull it tight, but not tight enough to cut into the stems or to break the wire.

FIGURE 9–6   *Tied flat spray construction. (a) Begin the spray by tying three fern fronds together with wire. (b) Place three flowers above the fern and tie them. (c) Place fern pillows in the center and sides to lift the flowers. (d) Add additional fern fronds to the sides of the spray to continue the length.*

Step 3: Place a flower stem on each piece of fern so that the fern tip extends about 6 inches beyond the flower head. The center flower will extend about 4 inches beyond those placed at the sides. Tie these stems with wire from the spool.

FIGURE 9–6(e)   Place flowers above each of the fern fronds used for background and pillows. (f) Complete the tied spray by adding the fern tails, filler flowers, and a bow at the base.

Step 4: Lay two pieces of filler fern (*Asparagus sprengerii* or *plumosus* fern) between the flowers to add depth to the spray. Tie the stems together with wire, as was done previously.

Step 5: Lay a single piece of flat fern in the center of the spray below the first flower so that the back of the foliage is facing upward. Fold the top of the fern frond down to meet the base of the stem. This will create a pillow for elevating the next flower to be placed upon it. Tie the fern and flower stem securely with wire.

Step 6: Next place a fern frond on each side of the center of the spray and slightly below the last flower stem on each piece of fern, as was done earlier. Then place filler fern between these flowers to fill the spaces. Tie all these stems securely with the wire.

Step 7: Form a pillow in the center of the spray from a piece of flat fern, as described in step 5. After placing the next flower stem on this pillow, tie the stems with wire.

Step 8: Place two additional fronds below the center pillow and on each side to form a background for the flowers. Place the flower stems on top of these fronds and then add filler fern between them. Again tie the stems with the continuous strand of wire from the paddle.

Step 9: Cut off the extraneous stems at a point about 6 inches below the area where the wires have been tied. Place two additional pieces of flat fern at the base of the spray stem facing downward with their stems wired to the main stem of the spray. These will appear as tails on the spray.

Step 10: Construct a bow from no. 120 metaline or no. 40 satin ribbon. Attach this to the spray with wire above the fern fronds, which were placed as tails on the spray.

Step 11: Complete the spray by cutting the wire from the spool and tying the free end securely within the spray.

The flat spray must be constructed tightly and securely so that it will not bend or flop when handled. The flowers and fern are wired about one-half the distance up the stems to form a strong central stem on the spray. The remaining stems located below the point of tying are broken and folded upward to add support to the center of the spray. Some floral designers construct the tied spray on a bamboo stake to achieve this support. Since the flower stems are no longer in contact with water, the sprays are wrapped in plastic while in the storage refrigerator and delivered to the funeral chapel on the day of the service.

Easel Pieces

The floral pieces displayed at a funeral service generally provide a background for the casket viewing area. Flat sprays are normally hooked onto large frames to provide a massed display of flowers. Bouquets and potted plants are placed on tables and pedestals to elevate them into view. Easels are used for mounting larger sprays and other miscellaneous designs to be displayed at a funeral service.

A florist easel consists of a tripod having two stationary legs and another that is movable from a flattened to an extended position. The movable leg can be laid flat for transporting the design. The floral piece may be mounted on the tripod by securing it to an accompanying hook or by using wires. The most common funeral easels are constructed in various sizes from heavy gauge green wire, or more decorative wooden frames are available.

Easel frames are used in funeral services to individually display the more unique and certain conventional designs. The larger double-end, standing sprays to be placed at the head or foot of the casket are mounted on the easel frame. Other floral pieces that are customarily displayed on easel frames include crosses, wreaths, and fraternal emblems.

Crosses: The Christian cross design is one of the more traditional funeral easel pieces (see Figure 9–7). It may be arranged as a simple cross in one or more colors, or it may have another design superimposed within it, normally at the intersection of the arms. Crosses may be constructed either from a styrofoam form or from dampened moss on a wire frame. To create a cross using moss, shredded sphagnum moss is thoroughly saturated with water. The moss is then squeezed to remove excess moisture and pressed into a firm ball as the wire frame is filled. When a generous amount of moss has been pressed into the wire frame, the entire moss surface is covered with green waxed paper from a 3-inch-wide roll (florists' waxed paper). This paper is cut when the frame is completely wrapped and the free end secured with a *greening pin* (florists' hairpin). The flower stems may then be easily picked through the paper and secured in the moss filler.

If the cross is to be formed from styrofoam, the standard dimensions are 21 inches in length by 18 inches in width at the crossarms. The cross is formed by first cutting a 2-inch thick sheet of styrofoam into 6-inch-wide strips with a saw. The longest strip is cut to a length of 21 inches and two 6-inch square pieces are also formed. These 6-inch pieces form the crossarms by placing them 6 inches from one end of the longest strip and securing them with wooden picks plunged through the plastic.

The styles of crosses used for funeral services may vary widely, depending upon the types of flowers used, complexity of the design, and the desires of the purchaser. A simple cross design constructed on a styrofoam support block is described next.

Step 1: Mount the styrofoam cross support block to an easel frame with the crossarms meeting at the point where the wire hook is located on the easel. Press the hook securely into the styrofoam block. Wire the block to the frame using a length of chenille wire that is pushed through the block from the front and twisted around the easel frame.

Step 2: Provide an edging of either net or satin around the outer perimeter of the cross by gathering the material into tight scallops secured with pins. Place this scalloped edging on the rear face of the cross and pin it so that the gathers will not be seen from the front.

Step 3: Remove individual flowers from their stems, place them on picks, and insert them into the front and sides of the cross to give a solid mass of flowers. Different types of flowers or flower colors may be used to differentiate the cross face from the edges. Pick and insert the flowers into the styrofoam block until the entire face and edges are covered.

FIGURE 9–7
A floral cross constructed
on an easel.

Step 4: For special emphasis, the designer may wish to create a cluster of flowers at the focal area. This is located at the intersection of the crossarms with the main axis of the cross. For best effect, the background flowers should all be one color. The accent design then may be of any other color and flower type. A small satin bow may be included in this area to coordinate the colors and add interest to the design.

Step 5: The keeping quality of this floral piece is markedly reduced when it is constructed without floral foam or water picks. Therefore, it is important to mist the entire surface of the design heavily with water and cover it with polyethylene plastic while it is in the storage refrigerator. The picked cross should not be delivered to the funeral chapel until the morning of the service.

Picked Wreaths: Wreaths used for funeral services are constructed in a manner similar to the cross. Generally, either a moss-filled wire frame or a preformed styrofoam circle is selected to serve as a support. Both

FIGURE 9–8
*A floral picked wreath
on an easel is often
used at funeral services.*

FIGURE 9–8
A floral picked wreath on an easel is often used at funeral services.

of these circular forms may be obtained from wholesale florists and supply firms in sizes ranging from 12 to 30 inches in diameter for funeral pieces.

The design and construction of a funeral wreath may vary widely. These differences in design styles will also influence the manner in which the flowers are secured to the frame. One of the most common wreath styles is that patterned after the Della Robbia style of Europe, where leaves are placed around the wreath in a pattern similar to the scales on a fish. Magnolia or lemon-leaf foliage is secured to the frame using greening pins. A cluster of flowers may then be placed in any of the quadrants on the wreath to create a focal area.

Another common design style includes wrapping the wreath frame with no. 40 or 120 ribbon. A small area is left free of ribbon to allow the construction of a floral focal point on the wreath. Net or lace edging may be added to the outside and inside portions of the circle and flowers added to fill out the wreath in other designs. The designer may use a great amount of creativity in styling wreaths for funeral services (see Figure 9–8).

FIGURE 9–9   *The Masonic Blue Lodge emblem with the corresponding color designations for flowers.*

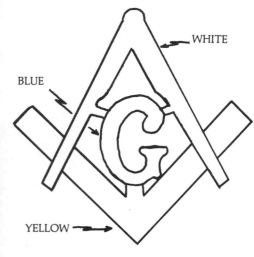

Fraternal Emblems

Whenever the deceased party was a member of a fraternal organization or lodge, that group will request that their insignia be used at the service. These emblems are constructed on styrofoam forms that create the shape of the design. Several of the more commonly used fraternal emblems that have specific requirements for their design include: the Blue Lodge Order of the Masonic Temple emblem, Eastern Star, Knights of Columbus, Moose, Elks, Eagles, and other organizations. Two of these popular emblem styles are discussed.

The Masonic Emblem: The Masonic Blue Lodge emblem depicts the carpenter's square and compass, with the letter G centered within the design (see Figure 9–9). The emblem may be purchased from a florist supply firm or it may be constructed from styrofoam sheets. Constructing the Masonic emblem must follow a rather rigid detail in design. The square must be exactly 90° with the arms directed upward. The compass always overlays the square, with the legs sharpened to a point and directed downward. This must be followed when the flowers are applied to the form.

FIGURE 9–10 *The emblem of the Order of Eastern Star and the color sequences for flowers.*

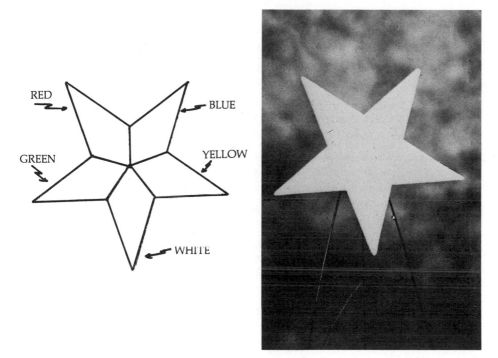

The flowers are generally picked onto the styrofoam base, using either wooden or steel picks or greening pins to secure them. The preferred colors are white for the compass, yellow for the square, and blue for the letter G. The letter G may be fashioned from a piece of styrofoam and spray painted or purchased from a wholesale florist firm. It is secured in the frame with wire or a wooden pick before the emblem is placed on a tripod easel.

Order of Eastern Star Emblem: The emblem for the Order of Eastern Star is formed in the shape of a five-pointed star. The colors used for the star points and their orientations must be closely followed. Flowers used on the star points going in a clockwise direction are: white, green, red, blue, and yellow. The white-colored star point is always mounted on the easel pointed downward (see Figure 9–10). The flowers are either dyed or sprayed with floral coloring tints whenever necessary. The unstemmed flowers are then placed on short picks and inserted into the styrofoam to form a solid mass on each star point. The finished emblem is then attached to the easel tripod with wire or chenille stems.

SERVICING THE FUNERAL

Funerals are solemn occasions where family members and friends pay their last respects to the deceased. The florist and all those personnel who are involved with the preparation and delivery of the funeral floral designs must also reflect this respect and solemnity to this occasion. The funeral services are generally preceded by a visitation period held the night before the actual service. For a Catholic service, a rosary service may follow the open visitation at the chapel. Many funeral directors insist that all floral tributes be delivered to the funeral chapel prior to the visitation period. The florist should be certain that all orders for funeral flowers are delivered at the scheduled times to satisfy the wishes of the funeral director.

When the flowers must be delivered to the funeral chapel the night before the service, the florist should construct as many of the floral designs as possible in water-filled containers or floral foam blocks. The picked and tied sprays or easel pieces will remain fresh for both the evening visitation and the morning funeral service, if given the proper care. These floral pieces should be constructed only from the freshest flowers that are in the optimum stage of maturity. The flowers should be properly conditioned before being arranged and the completed designs refrigerated until the time of delivery. Most funeral chapels are held overnight at reduced temperatures to provide more suitable conditions for the flowers. When flower orders are received after the deadline for delivery to the funeral chapel, other arrangements may be necessary. The florist could suggest that either a cut flower arrangement or a potted plant be delivered to the family home.

The delivery personnel at a flower shop have the responsibility for delivering and displaying the floral pieces at the funeral chapel. The floral designs are generally delivered to a side or rear entrance of the funeral chapel to avoid disrupting the normal business routine. The sprays, bouquets, potted plants, and easel pieces are carefully placed on their stands or racks and then arranged for their best display. The funeral chapel personnel will usually assist with the arrangement of the floral pieces. The delivery personnel should then refill all containers with water that were emptied before the delivery. Each of the floral designs should be inspected for damage and rearranged, if necessary, and the entire area cleaned of debris or water spills before leaving the chapel. This courtesy will help to ensure a continued business relationship between the funeral director and the florist.

Following the funeral service, the flowers may be taken to the cemetery for display at a graveside service. This is generally done by the funeral chapel personnel. Those floral designs that are most often taken to the cemetery include only the casket cover spray, flat sprays, and the easel pieces. The fresh flower bouquets and potted plants are usually taken to the family home. The florist shop personnel may be asked by the funeral director to assist in delivering these flowers.

SELECTED REFERENCES

BENZ, M. *Flowers: Geometric Form,* 3rd ed. Houston, Tex.: San Jacinto Publishing Company, 1966.

CUTLER, K. N. *How to Arrange Flowers for All Occasions.* Garden City, N.Y.: Doubleday and Company, 1967.

Floral Tributes, 4th ed. Lansing, Michigan: The John Henry Company, 1979.

McDANIEL, G. L. *Ornamental Horticulture.* Reston, Va.: Reston Publishing Co., 1979.

PFAHL, P. B. *The Retail Florist Business.* Danville, Ill.: Interstate Printers and Publishers, 1968.

SCANLON, J., and B. PALMER, eds. *Album of Designs: Funeral Flowers for Professional Floral Designers,* 22nd ed. Chicago, Ill.: Florists' Publishing Company, 1968.

TOLLE, L. J. *Floral Art for Religious Events.* New York: Hearthside Press, 1969.

STRATMAN, T. S. *Retail Floriculture, Book II: Designing and Care of Flowers and Foliage.* Ohio Agricultural Education Curriculum Materials Service. Columbus Ohio State University, 1976.

TERMS TO KNOW

Casket cover	Emblem	Malin	Water pick
Double-end spray	Foundation	Picking machine	Wooden pick
Easel	Lid spray	Saddle	

STUDY QUESTIONS

1. Explain why funeral flower orders are an important and necessary part of the retail florist business.
2. Explain why each funeral director should be consulted before designing funeral pieces to be delivered to the chapel. How might the funeral director's equipment and services influence the floral design styles created by the florist?
3. List the more common styles of floral pieces displayed at funeral services.
4. Discuss the obligations of the florist when servicing a funeral.

SUGGESTED ACTIVITIES

1. Invite a professional floral designer to your class to demonstrate the construction of funeral sprays and easel pieces.
2. Invite a funeral director to your class to discuss the use of flowers at funeral services. Discuss the proper methods for displaying flowers at funeral chapels.
3. Construct a double-end casket spray as a class project. Use any readily available flowers and greenery in constructing the spray. Discuss how the spray may be varied in shape to conform to different design styles.
4. Practice constructing tied flat sprays using easily obtained flowers.
5. Create various styles of crosses, wreaths, and easel pieces as a class project. Use styrofoam forms and pick the flowers into the support blocks.

GLOSSARY

Accent To call attention to a particular location in a floral design. To create emphasis in a design by use of a focal point.

Accented Neutral A color scheme that has one color predominating with a neutral blended with it. Neutral colors to be used are white, black, gray, or tan.

Accessory An item used in support of a floral design, such as a figurine, fruit, or candle.

Aesthetic Appearing to be pleasant; appreciative of beauty.

Aisleabra Candelabra that are attached to the ends of the church pews or seats on the main aisle for wedding ceremonies.

Aisle Runner A white carpet running the length of the aisle of a church sanctuary for wedding ceremonies.

Analogous A color scheme that utilizes any three adjacent hues (colors) from the color wheel.

Arm Bouquet A floral bouquet carried across the forearm for weddings or as a presentation bouquet.

Asymmetrical Balance Objects or flowers of unequal size, number, or visual weight placed on opposite sides of a vertical axis, as in an asymmetrical floral design style.

Balance A design principle. Placing objects in strategic locations to create a visual feeling of stability in a design.

Bent Neck A condition found on roses and other cut flowers when water can no longer enter the cut stem, causing the neck area to become weak and unable to support the flower.

Bloom (1) A term interchangeable with blossom. (2) The period of flower production on a plant.

Boutonniere A single flower or small assemblage of flowers worn by a man.

Broadleaf Evergreen Plants that retain their green leaves all year and possess large leaves. Not needle-bearing plants (conifers).

Butterfly A corsage accessory used as a filler between flowers. A net or lace section is folded in the center and a wire is attached for a stem.

Cage Holder A stem-anchoring device consisting of numerous openings in the surface to provide a method for supporting cut flower stems.

Cake Adapter A device used to support a floral foam block for arranging flowers that may be placed on top of a wedding cake.

Calyx A collective term for the sepals (flower bud leaves) of a flower. The calyx is generally green or leaflike, but may be colored or fused to form a cone around the petals.

Candelabra A fixture designed to support one or more candles for lighting. Used for special lighting effects for ceremonies such as weddings.

Canopy An arch or covering used at wedding ceremonies. The canopy is generally decorated with flowers and is used either at the altar (Chuppah) or at the rear of the church aisle.

Cascade Bouquet A bouquet style where the flowers are placed in a manner that allows them to hang below the main portion of the arrangement. Generally used as hand-held wedding bouquets.

Casket Cover A floral spray or decoration that is placed over the closed lid of a casket during a funeral service.

Center of Interest A term synonymous with accent or emphasis in design. Any object that attracts attention or creates a focal point in a design composition.

Centerpiece A floral arrangement that is placed in the center of a dining table or is used as an accent arrangement on a coffee table.

Chenille A wire stem covered by short, tufted cloth fibers. Popularly called a pipe cleaner.

Chroma A measure of the intensity of a color. The relative brilliance or softness (dullness) of a hue.

Circular Design A floral arrangement style that has a rounded form and may be viewed from any side.

Collarette A cardboard support placed behind gardenia flowers to protect the fragile petals when used in corsages.

Colonial Design A hand-held bouquet style that is constructed in a circular shape with an attached handle.

Color The visual interpretation of light waves from the visible spectrum. A design element that is synonymous with hue.

Color Wheel A diagram illustrating the various primary, secondary, and tertiary colors as they are applied to design.

Common Name The name by which a plant is generally known rather than by its scientific name.

Complementary Colors Any two colors (hues) located opposite each other on the color wheel when used together in a design.

Compote A stemmed container used for arranging flowers.

Condition (1) Quality of a flower or plant. (2) To prepare cut flowers by placing them in a refrigerated cooler in a floral preservative solution.

Consultation An interview conducted by a floral designer and a customer for the purpose of planning the floral decorations for a wedding ceremony or the funeral service of a family member.

Cool Colors Colors (hues) composed basically of blue and green tones.

Cornucopia A woven basket or other container designed in the shape of a goat's horn and shown spilling flowers or fruit. Also known as the horn-of-plenty.

Corsage Any grouping of flowers, net, bow, or other accessories to be worn by a woman.

Crescent A design form having the shape of a quarter moon.

Crosswire Method A technique used for adding stems to flowers for use in corsages. Two wires are inserted into the calyx at the base of the flower at 90° angles from each other. These wires are then folded downward and taped to create a stem.

Disbuds A term synonymous with standard flowers. Stems having all lateral flower buds removed leaving only a single, terminally placed flower.

Double-End Spray A floral spray constructed in an oval or double-triangular shape that is used as a funeral design.

Easel A three-legged stand constructed of either heavy wire or wood that is used to support and display wreaths, crosses, emblems, or floral sprays.

Elements of Design A term used to describe the function of the design principles and includes line, form, color, and texture.

Emblem Symbolic designs that depict the insignia of a fraternal organization or branch of military service.

Emphasis A design principle. The creation of a visual accent in a design.

Equilateral triangle A design form having the shape of a triangle with all sides of equal length.

Faience Finely glazed earthenware or pottery.

Fan A corsage accessory constructed from net or lace that is gathered along one edge and a wire stem attached.

Feathering The separation of a flower into several small florets for use in corsages.

Filler (1) A type of flower that is used to add interest and complete a design. (2) A material that is added to a container to anchor stems when designing.

Floral Cascade An individual portion of a cascade bouquet. It is created by fastening flowers and foliage to a central wire that is then attached to the central bouquet.

Floral Clay A water-proof, sticky material used in floral designing for such purposes as fastening stem-anchoring devices to containers.

Floral Foam A highly porous block used to support flower stems and hold water in an arrangement.

Floral Preservative A chemical mixture added to cut flower holding solutions to extend the life of the flowers.

Floral Tape A paraffin-coated paper that may be stretched over stems to firmly bind them together when creating corsages, wedding bouquets, or securing picked stems for arrangements.

Floret (1) A single flower in a flower head. (2) A smaller flower created by dividing a larger bloom into groups of petals.

Focal Point The location within a design attracting the greatest attention.

Form (1) A design term synonymous with shape or outline. (2) A type of flower having a distinctive shape.

Frond The leaflike structures of fern plants.

Garland An ornamentation fashioned from tinsel, flowers, or foliage into the shape of a wreath, chaplet, or roping.

Glamellia A traditional corsage made to resemble a camellia flower, ordinarily constructed from gladiolus petals.

Glamor Leaves Accessories used in corsages that are fashioned from fine material, net, lace, or beads to resemble foliage.

Glycerin Infusion A method for preserving foliage or flowers that keeps the plant material soft and pliable.

Greening Pins Wire pins having a U-shaped top that are used as fastening devices in flower arranging.

Hairpin Method A corsage wiring technique used for adding a stem to delicate, cup-shaped flowers such as tuberoses and stephanotis.

Hamper A container used for gladiolus and snapdragons that allows the flowers to remain upright during shipping.

Harmony A design principle. The successful blending of the design elements so that all components are compatible with the whole arrangement.

Hogarthian Curve A design having the shape of a modified S form, the upper portion using two-thirds of the figure and creating a free-flowing motion that leads the lines of the design to the focal point.

Hook Method A wiring technique where the wire is inserted through the flower head and a U-shaped hook created before the wire is pulled back into the petals.

Horizontal A design shape where the width exceeds the height.

Hue A design term having the same meaning as color.

Ikebana The art of Japanese floral arrangement. Literally interpreted as meaning "giving life to flowers."

Ikenobo (1) A Buddhist priest who established the first Japanese school of floral art. (2) Original Japanese floral art now called Ikebana.

Insertion Method A technique used for supporting a stem where the wire is inserted into the fleshy calyx below the flower head.

Intensity The visual quality of color created by adding gray. The brightness or dullness of flower petal color.

Jiyu-Bana The free-style design form of Japanese flower arranging that evolved after World War II.

Jushi A Japanese element of design that has the same meaning as Nejime.

Kenzan A Japanese stem-anchoring device that is similar to a needlepoint holder.

Latex The thick, milky sap found in some plant stems that causes plugging of the water-conducting tissues when used in arrangements.

Lid Spray A funeral floral design that is placed on the edge of an opened casket lid during a funeral service.

Liknon A Roman floral container consisting of a basket that was high at the back and flattened in front.

Line (1) A design element that defines the use of material in forming an outline or skeleton of an arrangement. (2) The Oriental style of design that utilizes arrangements having triangular shapes. (3) Flowers that create a linear outline in a design by being larger in one dimension than the other.

Line-Mass Arrangements The contemporary design style that combines the linear shapes with the massing of flowers at the focal area.

Malin A term that has the same meaning as paddle wire or wire that is wound on a short, flat piece of wood for use in designing.

Mass (1) A closely spaced grouping of flowers in an arrangement. (2) A flower form consisting of large petals or closely packed florets. (3) The European floral design style.

Metal Picks Metal picks with serrated points that are placed on stems by a machine and are used to anchor stems.

Miniatures Small, short-stemmed flowers arising from a central stem. Another term used for pixie carnation and sweetheart roses.

Modern Interpretive Design A free-form design style that does not utilize geometric shapes or flower masses.

Monochromatic A color scheme consisting of one color (hue) with its tints and shades.

Moribana A Japanese design style that is constructed in low, flat containers.

Nageire A Japanese design style that utilizes a curving form, rather than a triangular shape. These designs are normally constructed in upright containers.

Needlepoint Holder A stem-anchoring device used in flower arranging, consisting of many sharp-pointed spikes or nails. Also called a frog or pinholder.

Negative Space Balance in design created by the absence of flowers in one area being offset by flowers located in another.

Nejime A Japanese design element. Flowers or plant materials that are used as fillers or helpers for the main elements in a floral arrangement.

Neutral Colors Colors that are not located on the color wheel, but which influence those that are. Neutral colors are black, white, gray, and tan.

Nosegay A grouping of closely spaced flowers, net, and accessories in a hand-held floral arrangement. Also called a tuzzy-muzzy or a Colonial bouquet.

Orchid Pick A term having the same meaning as water pick. Used to provide water for orchid flowers when used in corsages. Also called a water tube.

Permanent Flowers Traditionally considered to be flowers constructed from polyethylene plastic, but more recently includes those created from silk or silk-like material, feathers, and dried flowers.

pH A measure of alkalinity or acidity. Measured as the negative logarithm of the hydrogen ion concentration of a solution.

Picking Machine A device used to secure metal picks to flower stems.

Pistil The female portion of a flower, consisting of the stigma, style, and ovary. Generally, a thick fleshy organ in the center of a flower.

Polychromatic A color scheme consisting of three or more unrelated hues.

Pompon A spray-type chrysanthemum having a flower shaped like a ball.

Preservative Chemicals added to vase water to aid in extending the life of cut flowers in arrangements.

Primary Colors The hues of red, yellow, and blue. Colors from which all other hues are derived.

Principles of Three The three main structural elements of a Japanese design, called Shin, Soe, and Tai.

Principles of Design Guidelines that govern the placement of flowers in designing floral arrangements.

Proportion A design principle. A pleasing relationship in size and shape of the parts of a design to the whole composition.

Puff An accessory used in corsages and wedding bouquets. Net or lace that has been gathered to form a series of folds to serve as a foundation for flowers.

Radiating Design A floral design having a fan shape and generally constructed of spike and mass flowers.

Relative Humidity A measure of the water vapor content of air expressed as the percentage required to reach saturation at a specific temperature.

Retail A business involved in selling products directly to the public.

Right Triangle An asymmetrical design style having a shape that approximates a right triangle.

Rikkwa (Rikka) The formal temple style of Japanese floral design, characterized by the massive, symmetrical arrangement of flowers in bronze ceremonial vases.

Rhythm A design principle. The creation of visual movement in a design.

Saddle A term used to describe the device used to hold a funeral spray that is placed on a casket cover.

Secondary Colors Hues created by mixing equal portions of any two primary colors. Secondary colors are green, orange, and violet.

Shade In design, the result of adding black to a color (hue). Flower petal shades are darker than the pure hues.

Shin The principle element of Japanese floral designs. The term has become known as the main stem that represents heaven in an arrangement.

Shin-O-Hana The early Buddhist temple floral art form of China.

Shokwa (Seika) Ancient Japanese floral style created by the Buddhist priest, Senchin. These designs were constructed in an asymmetrical style in low, flat containers.

Silica Gel A drying compound for use in drying flowers using the burial method.

Skeleton Flowers The primary flower placement in a design that establishes the outline of the arrangement.

Soe The secondary element of Japanese floral designs. It represents man in a Japanese design.

Sphagnum Sheet Moss Moss derived from the sphagnum plant that is used as a covering for planter soil and foam blocks in designs.

Spike Flowers Flower stems having a linear shape, generally with the more mature flowers at the base and buds at the tip (as in gladiolus).

Split-Complement A color scheme consisting of three colors on the color wheel; one hue used with each of those located on either side of its complement.

Spray (1) A cluster of flowers on a stem, as with pixie carnations or pompon chrysanthemums. (2) A floral decoration displayed at funeral services.

Stem Holder One of the various types of stem anchoring devices used in floral designing.

Styrofoam A rigid plastic foam material used as a stem-anchoring device and foundation for floral designs.

Support Blocks One of the various styles of floral foam or styrofoam blocks used as a stem support for floral arrangements.

Symmetrical Balance Objects or flowers of equal size or visual weight placed on opposite sides of a vertical axis, as in an equilateral triangle design style.

Symmetry Having the same elements or parts duplicated on each side of a vertical axis.

Tai The tertiary line of a Japanese design. It represents earth in an arrangement.

Tertiary Colors Hues obtained by mixing adjacent primary and secondary colors.

Texture Visual coarseness or softness of objects used as a design element.

Tint The result of adding white to a color. Flower petal color is lighter than the pure hue.

Tone A measure of the intensity of a color when diluted by gray.

Topiary In floral design, creating arrangements or bouquets in the shape of tiered balls.

Triad A color scheme consisting of any three colors located equidistant on the color wheel, such as red, blue, and yellow.

Tuft A corsage accessory constructed from net or lace material with an attached wire stem.

Tulle A type of decorative netting used as an accessory in corsage and wedding designs.

Tuzzy-Muzzy A small hand-held bouquet, originally designed to conceal a vial of smelling salts for young women in Europe and America.

Uke A Japanese design term that has the same meaning as Tai.

Unity A design principle. The blending of all parts of a design into a pleasing composition without a noticeable separation. Created by the repetition of the same flowers, colors, or textures throughout the design.

Value The degree of black or white added to a color to form its tint or shade. The lightness or darkness of the flower petal color.

Vertical Design An upright arrangement style that forms its main axis in a vertical line from the container.

Warm Colors Colors (hues) composed basically of yellow and red tones.

Water Picks Plastic or glass tubes that hold water and are topped with a rubber stopper. Flower stems are inserted through the stopper to reach the water in the tube. Water picks may possess a pointed base to allow them to be anchored in a support block.

Waxing A method used to prevent petals dropping from sensitive flowers, such as chrysanthemums. Liquid paraffin or wax is used to secure the petal bases on the flower calyx.

Wholesale Firms selling their products to retail businesses rather than to the general public.

Wilting The drooping of leaves or flowers caused by insufficient water in the cells.

Wooden Picks Short wooden sticks having a fine wire attached to one end that are used to anchor stems in foam support blocks.

Woodwardia Large stands of greenery that are used to provide a background for candles or floral bouquets; generally used for wedding decorations.

Wrapped-Wire Method A method for providing a stem or support for delicate flowers and foliage. The fine wire is carefully wrapped along the existing stem, doubled back along the stem, and then taped.

Wreath A circular arrangement of flowers, foliage, or other material that is generally used for holiday decoration or for funeral tributes.

Index